DANISH
CHAIRS

NORITSUGU ODA

CHRONICLE BOOKS
SAN FRANCISCO

First published in the United States in 1999 by Chronicle Books.

First published in Japan in 1996 by Korinsha Press & Co., Ltd.,
Tokyo, Japan.

Printed in Singapore.

Library of Congress Cataloging-in-Publication Data:

Oda, Noritsugu, 1949–
  Danish Chairs / Noritsugu Oda; preface by Takako Murakami.
    p.   cm.
  Includes index.
  ISBN 0-8118-2257-5
  1. Chairs—Denmark—History—20th Century—Catalogs.   I. Title.
NK2715.O29   1999
749'.32'094890904—dc21   98-8298
                                                 CIP

749.32 ODA

Cover and text design: PATRICIA**EVANGELISTA**

Photographs: YOSHIO**HAYASHI**

Translation: PATRICIA**YAMADA**

Distributed in Canada by
Raincoast Books
8680 Cambie Street
Vancouver, B.C. V6P 6M9

10 9 8 7 6 5 4 3 2 1

Chronicle Books
85 Second Street
San Francisco, California 94105

www.chroniclebooks.com

D

TABLEOFCONTENTS

PREFACE

I first visited Denmark in October 1968 at the end of the short autumn season. The sun, always low in the sky during the day—as if just about to set—dyed the rows of houses in Copenhagen, the capital, a dull yellow. This melancholy beauty reminded me of the way houses look in my native Japan. My experience of the long dark Danish winter, rather than of the mild summer with its luminous nights, taught me how to face and understand my own innermost nature.

As a Danish government scholarship student, I was privileged to be able to study at the Department of Furniture Design of the School of Architecture at the Royal Danish Academy of Fine Arts for two years, from 1968 to 1970. There I was introduced to the country and its culture. It was then, also, that I first encountered the timeless good taste of Danish furniture design. It made a lasting impression on me, both personally and professionally, and my own designs are rooted in my Danish experience.

In this book, Noritsugu Oda and I hope to show the essence and forms that constitute modern Danish design. The designs of these wonderful chairs are as fresh and functional today as when they were first conceived.

A BRIEF HISTORY OF MODERN DANISH FURNITURE DESIGN

A nation's way of living and thinking is marked by the local environment, the natural features of the land, and the nation's history. Consequently, since the goods made and used reflect a culture's spirituality, the various designs falling under the rubric of "Danish modern" express the heart and culture of the Danish people.

Denmark's school of furniture and crafts design is widely regarded as one of the greatest in the world. In its golden era from the 1920s through the 1960s, distinguished designers and craftspeople emerged from this school onto the international design scene, one after another. Even today, more than half a century later, a number of the furniture masterpieces from that era are being reproduced. Why is it that Denmark, of all countries, has led the way in twentieth-century furniture design? It seems to me that there is a unique quality to Danish modern design, and it is from this standpoint that I would like to speculate about the genesis of Danish modern furniture and, in particular, chairs.

THE CHARACTER OF DANISH MODERN FURNITURE

The creativity of the designer and the excellent technique of the craftsperson coalesce in Danish furniture. This applies both to handcrafted and mass produced furniture. The skills of the designer complement those of the maker and vice versa, and the comfort and needs of the users are considered whether the product is expensive or inexpensive. The high quality of the designs and the long life of the furniture produced create a feeling of intimacy for those who live with and use these products over many years. Danish design demonstrates a special understanding and use of the unique qualities of materials suitable for human needs. This reflects the Danes' experience of their natural environment as well as their creativity and innovation using traditional materials such as wood. These characteristics are present in all types of Danish designs, not only those for furniture. Materials are used in such a way as to produce timeless forms. Modern Danish furniture design is distinguished by excellent craftsmanship, a complete understanding of the materials used, an understanding of the functions of furniture in human life, a clear understanding and expression of beauty, respect for the creativity of the designer, and a dedication to quality of design and product.

DANISH DESIGN

How did good design come to be valued so highly by the Danish people? How did the sense of responsibility for creating functional as well as aesthetic designs develop among Danish designers? The slogan "a better life" has been used in many countries in many eras. Why was it that in Denmark at the beginning of the 1900s this phrase came to mean a higher standard of living, both materially and socially, for all social classes and served as the basis for a major movement that included architecture, interior design, and product design? At the heart of all types of Danish design is the conviction that the designer's mission is to supply products that enrich the lives of all the people and bring them into contact with beautiful, superior things that ensure better living. Several social movements swept the country in the nineteenth and twentieth centuries, resulting in this conviction. But why did this vision include establishing broader social rights for the populace? I believe that it came from the Danish people's highly sophisticated aesthetic values evolving from their particular way of life and spiritual background.

THE SOCIAL BACKGROUND OF DANISH DESIGN

In my research on the origins of the Danish design movement, I came across the Folk High School (Folkehojskole), one outcome of the Danish mass enlightenment movement. The founder of this movement, Nikolai Frederik Severin Grundvig (1783–1872), was a Lutheran pastor, composer of hymns, and a poet. His erudition was said to be the best in Scandinavia, and his influence on intellectual issues was widespread in Danish society. He was particularly interested in the education of tenant farmers and thought that all people should be given the opportunity to obtain an education. In 1833 and 1834, he published his educational philosophy. He supported the concept of adult education because he wanted people to consider themselves a part of something bigger and to become confident and industrious citizens. This, he believed, would be attained through the relationship of teacher and student, students' interactions with each other, and the study of history, poetry, and music. His ideals were realized by Kristen Kold (1816–70) and became the educational standards of the Folk High School that ran a winter course for young boys and a summer course for girls. Students came to this school of their own initiative and paid their own study and living expenses.

In 1864, after overcoming various obstacles, the Folk High School emerged as a source of national energy and assumed an important place in the culture of the Danish people. By 1980, ninety-one of these schools had been established nationwide, and the Folk High School continues to be an influential form of education. Danish culture believes its national high school to be a major part of its cultural inheritance, where educational and democratic experiments take place and where the potential for the future is explored. This type of schooling has been a crucial factor in the development of the Danish people's acute sense of aesthetics. As early as the 1830s the need for educating the ordinary people had been discussed and the Folk High School was established in 1844 to answer this need. Universal education was not just the idea of intellectuals; farmers and townspeople shared this belief. The spiritual and economic support that would make it possible for all classes of people to obtain an education was already present. The success of this Danish educational system reflects the Danish commitment to high standards of value. Surprisingly, this autonomous, noncompulsory education has existed for 150 years without a break. To bring this about, it was necessary that the economic status of the common people reach a standard that would allow them to obtain an education. The Farmers' Cooperative Association started in order to improve the lives of farmers, but it had a wider, beneficial impact on the lives of all Danish people, indirectly supporting the development of the Folk High School. Established about 1880, the Farmers' Cooperative Association played a major role in the development of Danish agriculture. In that era of small farms, the association exported agricultural products, thus gaining power and status among farmers and throughout the Danish economy. Because it handled most of the exportable agricultural products produced, it gained strong support from the farmers and became the core organization for bettering the economic and social conditions of the small farmers. The association established its own savings bank in 1851, and retail sales were started in 1866 by Hans Christian Sonne at Chisted Juran. The retail sales arm of the association spread rapidly in urban areas; 400 shops had been opened by 1890 and 1526 shops by 1913. The retail sales section became powerful within the association by buying agricultural products and other goods produced by the members and then reselling them. This eventually led to further expansion. Mechanization and industrialization accelerated the export of such items as butter and eggs; even small farmers could now produce on a larger scale and thereby obtain greater economic benefits. As the cooperative movement continued to expand, a cooperative bank was opened. In 1904, a sanatorium was established for members, further demonstrating the association's wide concern for human beings and the quality of their lives. It next entered the areas of publishing, movie making, and theater. Then, in 1932, a noncompulsory school that provided technical and general cultural education was founded. This brief history summarizes how the Farmers' Cooperative Association was instrumental in promoting better social as well as economic values.

Another social movement was important in heightening social consciousness and values. The daily life of every country is largely in the hands of its women. The women's movement that began in Denmark in the 1800s, at about the time of the Folk School and Farmers' Cooperative movements, had as its purpose obtaining equal status with men in the family, society, and nation. A Danish Women's Citizens Association was established in 1871 to upgrade the status of unmarried women, who had a very low place in the society of that time. The association worked to establish the rights of women to be educated, to vote, and to stand as candidates for election. After overcoming a number of setbacks, a school for women was established between 1872 and 1876. Other rights secured included entrance to the university in 1875, participation in local elections in 1908, and voting privileges in national elections in 1915. The equalization of parental rights followed in 1922, and the rights of husbands and wives in 1947. The women's movement not only gained social rights for women, it revolutionized the way women thought about themselves and Danish society. Equal status with men in the work force, society, home, and nation allowed Danish women to pursue active roles in changing the structure of society and enriching themselves as human beings.

These three important social movements—the Folk High School, the Farmers' Cooperative Association, and the women's movement—show that from early in the last century Denmark has had influential groups that promoted public interest and contributed to the betterment of life for all the people. These organizations and social movements laid the groundwork for the high standards that the Danish people today expect from their designers, craftspeople, and furniture makers.

At the beginning of the twentieth century, Danish furniture design was still closely associated with the styles of other European countries, particularly those of France and England, and the furniture produced was mainly for the use of the upper classes. A nascent school of Danish furniture design, however, did exist. Gradually it developed a sophisticated neoclassical style that was not merely imitative and that showed a consciousness of what constitutes quality and good craftsmanship. As early as 1770 the Danish Royal Academy of Fine Arts adopted a written examination for furniture designers. It tested students and craftspeople on the principles of drafting as well as on the quality of their products. Licenses were granted to those who passed the examination. Everyone involved in the various fields of design—craftspeople and furniture makers as well as designers and architects—was expected to develop a discerning eye and an aesthetic sense. Apprentices training under masters were also required to study drafting and go on to the Academy. The beautiful and sophisticated pieces of neoclassic furniture designed by C. F. Harsdoff in the last decades of the eighteenth century are examples of what the Academy sought to achieve.

The Royal Furniture Trading Association, established in 1777, played a major role in promoting traditional forms of craftsmanship. As well as actual guidance on furniture making, it provided members access to excellent quality woods, drawings, and three-dimensional models, thereby setting standards of quality for product design. G. E. Rosenberg, a student of the French architect N. H. Jardine, was the first manager of this institute and was influenced by French ideas. His successor, C. Anker, was strongly influenced by English furniture traditions. During this early period foreign styles served as the foundation of Danish furniture design. Other eminent leaders during its early years were N. Abiligaad and G. Bindesboll. The desire for and production of sophisticated goods of excellent quality and craftsmanship contributed to the success and growth of the Royal Furniture Trading Association. However, in 1815, the association was disbanded because of severe economic recession.

Another group influential in the history of Danish design was the Copenhagen Furniture Industry Cooperative Association, formed in 1554. It had a shop where participating furniture makers could sell their products. This association continued to raise the quality of craftsmanship and products and became the prototype of later Danish furniture design groups. The first shops were established in 1780 and even in times of economic and social difficulties, such as during the heavy industrialization that took place throughout Europe after World War I, it continued to exhibit products made by individuals as well as those made in furniture workshops. The existence and activities of this cooperative prevented the decline in quality and the disappearance of craftsmanship that occurred in other European countries.

THE GENESIS OF DANISH MODERN DESIGN

The seemingly sudden blooming of Danish furniture and crafts designs in the twentieth century actually was the flowering of the events of several centuries. Many innovative young Danish designers became active in the 1920s. Indeed, throughout Europe, there was extensive experimentation in many areas of art: painting, sculpture, architecture, and crafts. In England, at the end of the nineteenth century, the arts and crafts movement led by John Ruskin and William Morris sought to reinstate in craftsmanship standards of quality and aesthetics that had been lost during the Industrial Revolution. The Deutscuher Werkbund was formed in Munich in 1907, and Le Corbusier, who published *Things After Cubism* in 1915, became the leader of the *espirit* nouveau movement in France. In the Netherlands, Theo van Doesburg and Piet Mondrian published the avant-garde art magazine *De Stijl*, which had a deep impact both on abstract art and the design movement. Then in 1919 Walter Gropius founded the Bauhaus in Germany and the concept of minimalism swept through Europe.

The innovative ideas promulgated by these movements were widely heralded in the Scandinavian countries. As if in response to these new directions, novel theories of art took hold, particularly in Sweden. Gregor Paulsson was active in areas ranging from art history and design to urban sociology. He developed a consistent, comprehensive theory of plastic art that had far-reaching impact. Paulsson was a great functionalist theoretician, and he was the major instigator of the revolution in architecture and craft design that took place in northern Europe during the 1920s and 1930s. His motto, "better goods for daily life," which had been used in 1919 by the Swedish Craft Institute as a slogan for the design movement in that country, became a catch phrase in the other Scandinavian countries. Paulsson's theoretical position on design was a psychosociological one based on his extensive research on how "meaning" comes into being, and his study of the structure of style placed great importance on its social dimension. He saw art not simply as the abstract development of style but as a complex of many functions, and viewed it as the outcome of social conditions. He accepted the spirit of functionalism but added a sociological dimension by taking into account the needs of the consumer.

According to Paulsson, the designer's mission was to achieve three aims: make beauty concrete (the aesthetic factor), create practical goods (the utilitarian factor), and educate the consumer (the social factor). People should be given a choice of products that would balance life styles and nature. Not only should designers have an understanding of utility and beauty, but also a sense of what is of real value to consumers. In 1956 Paulsson, together with his son Niels, published *Thingens bruk ock pragel* (The form of a thing and its use). In it, he sets forth his aesthetic-functionalist theory in language intelligible to the layperson.

After he visited the 1925 Paris International Exposition, Paulsson made a proposal that proved instrumental in setting up the Stockholm Exposition of 1930. This exposition is said to be the beginning of "functionalism" in northern Europe. Its theme was "Housing, Traffic, and Furniture," and it served as a showcase for Paulsson's ideas of how future industrial development should serve the needs of the growing middle class.

Gunnar Aspland, the architect who was in charge of planning the exhibition's buildings, created an international style (from which functionalist architecture emerged) that differed radically from his previous works. The architecture of these buildings had a deep impact on the young Danish designers of that time. The concepts of functionalism and international style, earlier proposed by Gropius and Le Corbusier, entered northern Europe at this exposition. In Denmark, however, the form that functionalism took was related to the particular concerns and needs of Danish society.

THE YOUNG DANISH DESIGNERS OF THE 1920s

The young Danish designers who embraced functionalism in the early twentieth century chose a path different from that taken by the Bauhaus school. This was beneficial to subsequent Danish design in that the works produced exhibited distinct aesthetics and function from those produced in other European countries. The modern design movement originating in Denmark was made up of several branches. The architects who established the avant-garde journal *Kritisk Revy* (Criticism) showed a social as well as an artistic philosophy. They attacked artistic classicism for losing track of the needs of human beings. This journal printed critiques not only of architecture but also of various types of design and craft products and called for designers to show a greater social conscience and concern for the consumer. The magazine's editor, Poul Hennigsen, noted that the type of everyday goods used affected the quality of family life, as did the layout of the house. He stated that it was the moral duty of designers to be concerned about the quality of people's lives. Because the present ceramics and furniture industries did not deal with this concern, he claimed, they were of no help for improving people's lives. The journal ceased publication in 1928, but its issues provide a fascinating record of the early history of Danish functionalism. During its period of publication, it exerted great influence for change. Young designers became conscious of the importance of the social roles of their professions and of the need for those in the arts to lead the way in promoting better ways of living.

The establishment in 1924 of the Department of Furniture Design in the School of Architecture of the Royal Danish Academy of Fine Arts and Kaare Klint's teaching career there were of great significance to twentieth-century Danish furniture design. Both an architect and designer, Klint became a major force in art education. He was a very strict but extremely charismatic teacher. The curriculum of the Department of Furniture Design developed from Klint's personal philosophy of design. From its inception, the department set high standards for Danish furniture design, and its influence remained strong for several decades. Klint educated many furniture designers of later renown with a combination of theoretical and practical concepts. The course started with the students measuring examples of "good" chairs. This taught them to understand both the scale of furniture and the scale of the human body on which the design and construction of chairs are based. They then learned how to harmonize the scales of the things that are used in combination with furniture (lamps, vases, plates, et cetera) and the scale of pieces of furniture in a group. They also measured the human body and adjusted the scale of the furniture designed to its dimensions.

In hindsight, these practices may seem obvious and logical, but what Klint was teaching in 1917 was revolutionary. Today this is called "modularization"; but, considering that it was only in 1948 that Le Corbusier popularized the term "modular," it is clear that many of Klint's ideas were far ahead of his time. Moreover, in assessing the types of furniture produced through the ages, he found particular beauty and rationality in the English furniture designs of the eighteenth century, and he had his students measure chairs designed by Chippendale and others. This attitude of learning from past masterpieces continues to be an important aspect of modern Danish design.

Looking at Klint's contribution to Danish furniture design, we see that he taught his students to measure things actually used in daily life; to take into consideration the scale of the human body and its movements; to investigate the structure, usage, and handling of the materials to be used; to inquire into the nature of aesthetics; and to work in close collaboration with furniture makers. Many of those he educated enthusiastically passed on his ideas, and a Klint "school" appeared. In addition, as their individual talents developed, Klint's students became the leading furniture designers of the next generation. It is their designs that gained international renown and are thought of as "Danish modern."

THE IMPORTANCE OF THE FURNITURE INDUSTRY ASSOCIATION'S EXHIBITIONS

The annual exhibitions of the Furniture Industry Association, which took place from 1927 to 1966, provided a place where young designers could show products that demonstrated their talents. These exhibitions were instrumental in Danish furniture gaining a strong international reputation. From the beginning, the public was shown items of superb craftsmanship that came from the workshops of various cabinetmakers, and consumers were exposed to high quality, functional, handcrafted furniture. In 1927, the furniture maker Henrik Wörts exhibited some examples of simple, low-cost living room furniture made of oak that particularly appealed to the general public. The popularity of this furniture stemmed from its simplicity and the high quality of the material used. Because of the public interest generated by designs such as Wörts's, the exhibition became an annual one.

At the first exhibition only three designers, Kaj Gottlob, Otto Meyer, and Helweg Møller, showed furniture produced in collaboration with furniture workshops. The furniture makers were quick to recognize the importance of collaboration and soon were exhibiting what they considered their best collaborative pieces. Moreover, a competition for new designs and styles was organized, and this led to the establishment of long-term relationships with young designers. Because the exhibition was an annual one, the design competition served to bring fresh ideas to furniture making and craftsmanship.

At the second exhibition, Viggor Sten Møller, Kaare Klint, and Kaj Gottlob presented exceptional pieces of furniture based on novel designs. Because of this long-term collaboration between the furniture makers and the young designers, a new design movement was born in which superior handcrafted furniture was created for the general consumer rather than for a rich elite. This in turn created the need for a modern furniture industry. Many prestigious designers chose to exhibit their masterpieces at Danish modern furniture shows. The importance of this annual exhibition can not be overestimated.

In 1930 Kaare Klint showed a cupboard with a design based on the measurements of the dishes and cups meant to be stored in it and, in addition, a Faaborg chair. Both had been designed in 1917, but they were representative of Danish functionalism, systematization, and modularization, as well as being examples of Klint's concept of rational beauty. That same year the designer Mogens Voltelen also participated, and Ole Wanscher participated in 1931, Arne Jacobsen in 1932, Acton Bjørn in 1933, Mogens Koch in 1935, Finn Juhl in 1937, Hans J. Wegner in 1938, Børge Mogensen in 1939, Ejner Larsen in

1942, Nanna Ditzel in 1944, Poul Kjærholm in 1952, Arne Karlsen in 1958, and Jørgen Gammelgaard in 1960. Those named are a small portion of the more than 230 designers who participated in this exhibition during the forty years of its existence. In addition, more than ninety furniture makers, including A. J. Iversen, Johannes Hansen, and Niels Vodder, took part.

Furniture maker–designer pairs included Rudolf Rasmussen and Kaare Klint; A. J. Iversen and Ole Wanscher; E. Rasmussen and Børge Mogensen; Johannes Hansen and Hans J. Wegner; and Niels Vodderand and Finn Juhl. These long collaborative relationships enhanced the techniques and artistic senses of both the designers and furniture makers and led to Denmark's entrance into the international furniture market. The Furniture Industry Association's exhibitions therefore not only had great impact on modern furniture design, they laid the foundation for one of the country's most important export industries. Because of these exhibitions, the world came to know twentieth-century Danish furniture and the names of the men who made it.

DEN PARMANENTE

The remarkable advances in Danish furniture design that occurred during the 1930s stimulated other craft goods used in daily life and generated what became a widespread modern design movement. Kay Bojesen was the chief driving source of this movement. He trained under the internationally renowned silversmith Georg Jensen, who was known for his handcrafted, superbly designed silver products. Bojesen's belief that one's own inner sense should be expressed in accordance with the qualities of the materials used stood in opposition to the manufacturing principles of the time. The simple lines of his silver goods embody functional beauty and convey the essence of his designs. They prove that beauty, function, and simplicity need not be contradictory. Many designers of the time, including Bojesen working in silver, Nathalie Krebs and Axel Salto in ceramics, Marie Gudme Leth in textiles, transcended the boundaries of traditional Danish design by their use of novel concepts. The design movement of which they were a part was concerned with all aspects of human life, and the products they produced had consequences for Danish furniture design as well. Then in 1931 Kay Bojesen and Christian Grauballe established Den Parmanente, a permanent site for the exhibition and sale of Danish crafts and furniture.

Bojesen, who believed that true craftsmanship and design should point the way for industrial designs, wrote extensively about these new concepts for silversmiths and designers in other fields. Grauballe, the managing director of Holmegaards Glasværk, understood aesthetics as well as the management of business and agreed with Bojesen. By combining their abilities, these two men successfully guided the new design movement artistically and economically through Den Parmanente, which became the premier exhibition space. To exhibit there required fresh, challenging ideas that produced a tension between the desire and the finished product. This competitive consciousness resulted in the creation of highly sophisticated functional furniture and crafts. Various goods—

ceramics, furniture, toys, interiors, textiles, and metal work—came to be classed as products of Danish modern design.

Den Parmanente's shop on Vesterport Street, the commercial center of Copenhagen, extended its influence. People from countries throughout the world visited the exhibition rooms, and the name Den Parmanente became an international byword. After the closing of the Furniture Makers Guild Exhibitions in 1966, Den Parmanente became even more important in the development and marketing of Danish crafts and furniture. It continued to have a leading role until 1981. That year the annual Scandinavian furniture fair was established in Beracenter, the Danish International Furniture Fair was held in Fredlicia, and the Furniture Makers Autumn Exhibition was begun. By 1988, its pre-eminent role was greatly diminished by these other annual exhibition-sales, and Den Parmanente was closed.

CONCLUSION

Danish furniture gained international renown not only because of support from the Danish government and royal family but because it satisfied basic human needs. The reasons for its continued excellence are complex and involve not only form and design, but a far-reaching understanding of traditional wood-working and modern engineering techniques, economic factors, the presence of highly trained craftspeople, and the unparalleled creativity of its designers and their recognition of consumers' needs and desires. Fortunately, throughout the twentieth century Denmark has been able to provide all these conditions. From 1920 to 1970 the Danish design movement pioneered new techniques in the use of wood and promoted the education of craftspeople and designers. New types of imported wood for furniture and national and international exhibitions kept the movement vibrant. The comprehensive education given furniture designers and the prizes offered for excellence of design stimulated creativity and bestowed honor and status. All of these factors led to an unprecedented output of furniture and craft goods from a culture that values designs that create better ways of living for human beings.

A FEW NOTES TO THE READER

1. The caption information is listed in the following order:
    > the materials used to make the chair
    > the measurements for the chair listed in inches (width x depth x height), seat height, and weight in pounds
    > the measurements for the chair listed in millimeters (width x depth x height), seat height, and weight in kilograms
    > the name of the manufacturer

2. The year given for the chair designs often vary according to source. In this book, the author has used the most widely used and/or accepted dates.

3. The schematic illustrations were created by the author and drawn at a scale of $1/5$. The reduction ratio in this book is $1/10$ of the original dimensions.

THE CHAIRS

KAARE**KLINT**

[PROFESSOR, ARCHITECT, DESIGNER] **1888–1954**

KAARE KLINT

Kaare Klint became a painter's apprentice in 1903. He attended technical school at Møller Jensen's Art School and Krøyer's Art School. He entered the Royal Danish Academy of Fine Arts, where he studied under Carl Petersen. He then became a professor of building design at the Academy. After working as a painter for several years, he opened his own office as an architect in 1922. He developed a system of standard dimensions from his research in the physical stature and dimensions of the human body and the tools and implements used in everyday life. He also combined the dignity of eighteenth-century English furniture with the simple, rational casualness of modern times. These innovations strongly influenced the Danish design world. In 1924 he established the Furniture Department at the School of Architectural Design, the Royal Danish Academy of Fine Arts. While serving as professor of building design at the Academy, he taught many students who would go on to become well-known designers in their own rights and is thus considered the founder of modern Danish furniture design.

HONORS> Eckersberg Medal, 1928. Grand Prix, World Exposition in Barcelona, 1929, and Brussels, 1935. Bissen Prize, 1938. Royal Designer of Industry, London, 1949. C. F. Hansen Medal, 1954.

MATERIALS> Mahogany, Rosewood, Cane
24^{19}/$_{32}$ x 25^{13}/$_{16}$ x 36^{13}/$_{32}$ / Sh 17^{3}/$_{16}$ in. / 25.96 lbs.
615 x 645 x 910 / Sh 430 mm / 11.8 kg
MANUFACTURER> Rud. Rasmussens Snedkerier Aps.

This chair is a redesign of an eighteenth-
century English chair. The original chair had
small casters. Except for this one point,
Klint's chair is a faithful model. The chair
has beautifully inlaid rosewood arms and is
still in production.

DESIGNER(S)>
KAARE KLINT

NAME>
EASY CHAIR №4488

YEAR>
1932

MATERIALS> Mahogany, Cane
27¹⁹/₃₂ x 25¹⁹/₃₂ x 28¹³/₁₆ / Sh 17¹⁹/₃₂ in. / 15.4 lbs.
690 x 640 x 720 / Sh 440 mm / 7.0 kg
MANUFACTURER> Rud. Rasmussens Snedkerier Aps.

The Faaborg Museum in Faaborg City, Funen, is made up mainly of Matz Rasmussen's collection of Funen folk art. This chair was designed by the architects Carl Petersen and Kaare Klint for that museum. Several different variations of this chair were made between 1914 and 1923.

Kaare Klint / Faaborg chair / 1914–23 / Rud. Rasmussens Snedkerier Aps.

Kaare Klint / Arm chair / 1923 / Rud. Rasmussens Snedkerier Aps.

DESIGNER(S)>
KAARE KLINT

NAME>
FAABORG CHAIR

YEAR>
1914

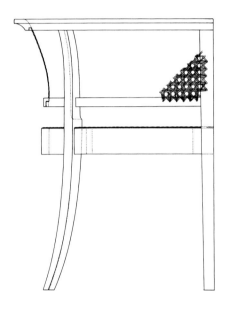

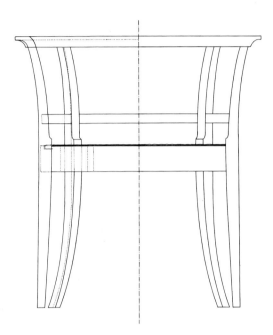

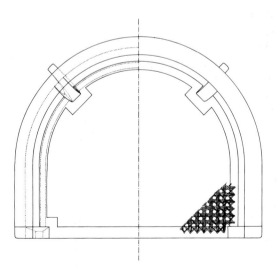

FAABORG CHAIR

MATERIALS> Mahogany, Leather
22^{13}/$_{16}$ x 22^{3}/$_{16}$ x 35^{13}/$_{32}$ / Sh 18 in. / 18.92 lbs.
570 x 555 x 885 / Sh 450 mm / 8.6 kg
MANUFACTURER> Rud. Rasmussens Snedkerier Aps.

The name of this chair comes from the color of the seat. Because it was awarded a prize at the Barcelona Exposition of 1929, it also is called the Barcelona Chair. The famous Barcelona Chair designed by Mies van der Rohe was exhibited at the same exposition. This chair shows the influence of the famous English furniture maker Thomas Chippendale.

Kaare Klint / Dining chair / 1927 / Rud. Rasmussens Snedkerier Aps.

DESIGNER(S)>	NAME>		YEAR>
KAARE KLINT	RED CHAIR OR BARCELONA CHAIR	N$^{\underline{o}}$ 3758A	1927

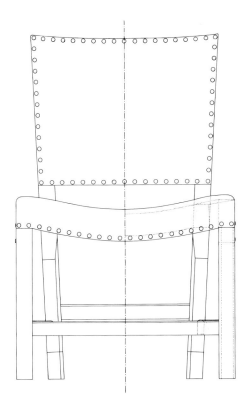

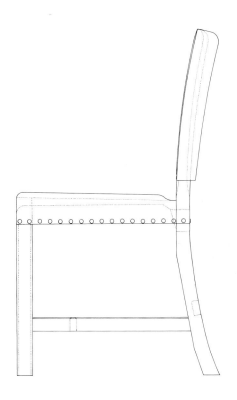

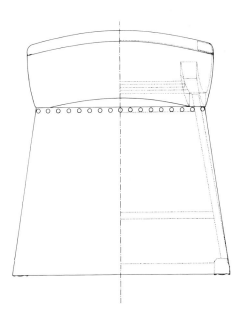

MATERIALS> Ash, Canvas
23³/₁₆ (1⁷/₈) x 19¹⁹/₃₂ x 17³/₁₆ (28¹⁹/₃₂) in. / 6.05 lbs.
580 (47) x 490 x 430 (715) mm / 2.75 kg
MANUFACTURER> Rud. Rasmussens Snedkerier Aps.

The Propeller Stool derived its name from the
unique curves of the legs, which give them a
propeller shape. When the stool is folded up the
legs and the brace form a single, round bar.
Thus, the frame of this work gives the appearance of being created from the curved faces of
a single shaft.

| DESIGNER(S)> | NAME> | | YEAR> |
| KAARE KLINT | PROPELLER STOOL | Nº 8783 | 1927 |

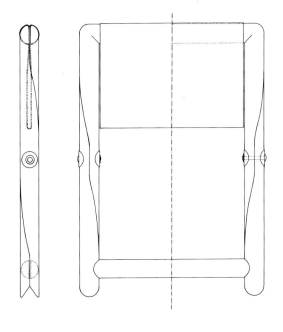

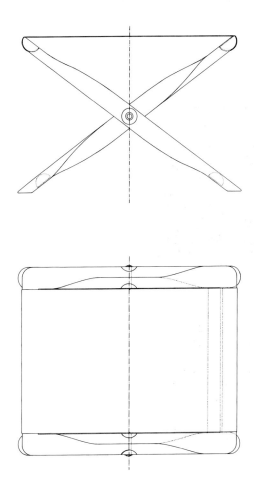

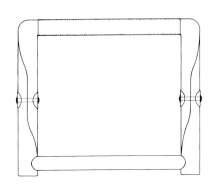

NAME>

PROPELLER STOOL   Nº 8783

MATERIALS> Ash, Canvas
22¹³/₁₆ x 22¹³/₁₆ x 32 / Sh 13³/₁₆ in. / 14.3 lbs.
570 x 570 x 800 / Sh 330 mm / 6.5 kg
MANUFACTURER> Rud. Rasmussens Snedkerier Aps.

The basis for the design of this chair was a colonial chair used by the English army in India. The knockdown construction was designed for easy carrying. Greatly influenced by this chair design, Swedish designer Arne Norrel designed a similar chair.

Ole Wanscher / Safari chair / c. 1940 / maker unknown

DESIGNER(S)>	NAME>	YEAR>
KAARE KLINT	SAFARI CHAIR STOOL	1933

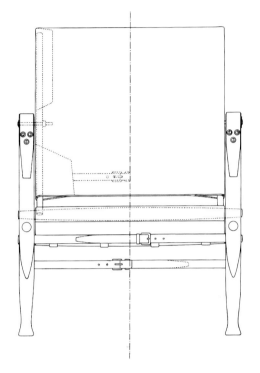

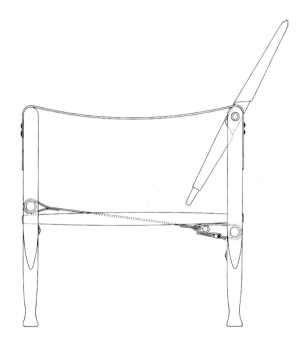

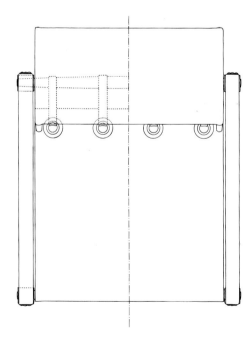

MATERIALS> Teak, Cane, Canvas
23³/₁₆ x 57¹³/₁₆ x 36 / Sh 14 in. / 27.5 lbs.
580 x 1445 x 900 / Sh 350 mm / 12.5 kg
MANUFACTURER> Rud. Rasmussens Snedkerier Aps.

Klint created this chair as a redesign of the familiar, classic deck chair. The seat is rattan. The leg rest folds under the seat, and the chair itself folds in half, making it convenient for storage. Klint's chair is probably the most beautiful deck chair currently in production.

Børge Møgensen / Deck chair / c. 1966 / A/S Søborg Møbelfabrik

DESIGNER(S)>	NAME>	YEAR>
KAARE KLINT	DECK CHAIR № 4699	1933

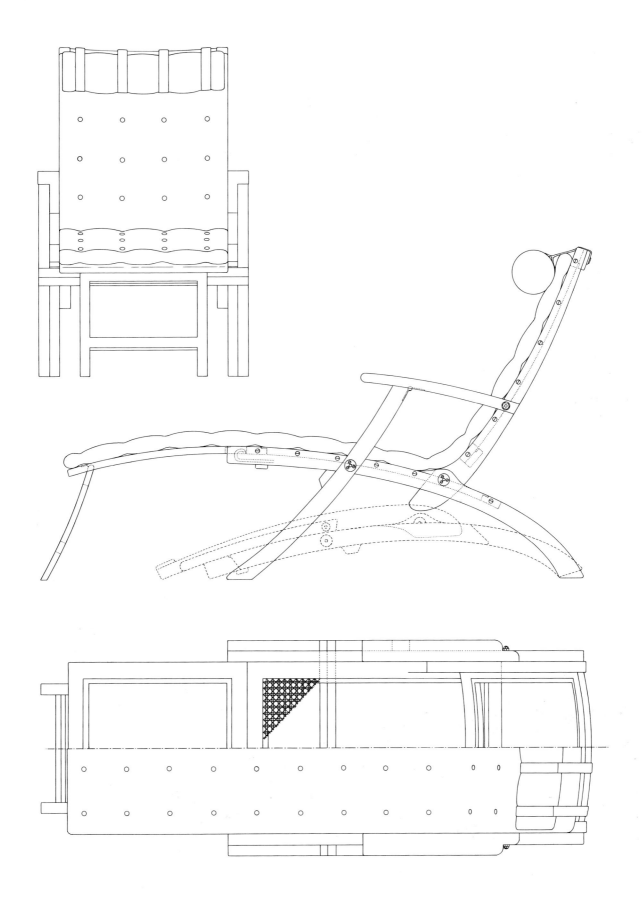

NAME>

DECK CHAIR № 4699

KAJ**GOTTLOB**

[PROFESSOR] **1887–1976**

KAJ GOTTLOB

Graduated from the Technical School and the Royal Danish Academy of Fine Arts. Worked with Hack Kampmann, 1908-1920. Opened his own office in 1920. Teacher at the Royal Danish Academy of Fine Arts, School of Architecture, 1924-1938. Architectural Inspector at the Royal Court, 1936.

HONORS> Gold Medal of the Royal Academy, 1915.

MATERIALS> Oak, Cane Fabric
$25^{13}/_{16}$ x $24^{3}/_{16}$ x $34^{19}/_{32}$ / Sh $18^{13}/_{16}$ in. / 23.44 lbs.
645 x 605 x 865 / Sh 470 mm / 10.2 kg
MANUFACTURER> maker unknown

In the world of Danish architecture and interior design, furniture design is carried out primarily by one of three types of artists—architects, specialists in furniture design, and artists known as "snedkermasters," who have been placed in charge of the craftsmen actually making the furniture. This chair was designed by Kaj Gottlob, a noted architect who also served as professor at the School of Architecture of the Royal Danish Academy of Fine Arts.

DESIGNER(S)>	NAME>	YEAR>
KAJ GOTTLOB	ARM CHAIR	UNKNOWN

KAY**FISKER**

[PROFESSOR] **1893–1965**

KAY FISKER

Kay Fisker worked under Anton Rosen from 1912 to 1916 and under Hack Kampmann from 1918 to 1919. He graduated from the Royal Danish Academy of Fine Arts, Architecture Department, in 1920 and opened his own office as an architect. He served as editor of the magazine *Arkitekten* from 1919 to 1927. Beginning in 1919, he served as instructor and then assistant professor at the Royal Danish Academy of Fine Arts, where he was granted a full professorship in 1936. He had great influence and played an auspicious role in the development of the Danish architectural world. From 1936 to 1942 he designed furniture for the Copenhagen Co-op and served as the director of the Denmark Arts and Crafts Museum.

HONORS> Gent City Gold Medal, 1921. Eckersberg Medal, 1928. C. F. Hansen Medal, 1947.

MATERIALS> Beech, Fabric
30 x 31³/₁₆ x 35¹³/₃₂ / Sh 18 in. / 52.36 lbs.
750 x 780 x 885 / Sh 450 mm / 23.8 kg
MANUFACTURER> maker unknown

Kay Fisker was a well-known professor of architecture at the Royal Danish Academy of Fine Arts and produced exquisite silverware. The year this chair was made and the craftsman who made it are unknown. The design of the chair, however, suggests that it was designed sometime between 1930 and 1940.

DESIGNER(S)>	NAME>	YEAR>
KAY FISKER	WINGBACK CHAIR	1930–40

JACOB**KJÆR**

[SNEDKERMASTER, DESIGNER] **1896–1957**

JACOB KJÆR

Jacob Kjær studied as a joiner under his father's tutelage. He was certified as a journeyman joiner in 1915 and received the silver medal the same year. From 1918–20 he studied at the Institute of Arts and Crafts Museum in Berlin. From 1921–24 he worked in Paris as a joiner, and in 1926 he returned to Copenhagen where he opened his own workshop. His career as a highly skilled furniture craftsman eventually sparked his talents as a designer. His furniture designs are characterized by a quiet simplicity enhanced by the craftsman's understanding of the materials used. In particular, his chairs display gentle curves elegantly accented by the contrast between the lovely wooden finishes and the leather binding techniques at which he excelled. The harmony between these elements became a trademark of his style. His craftsman's knowledge and understanding of the materials allowed him to develop such natural forms while maintaining a careful control over every minute detail.

Jacob Kjær was one of the few designers truly able to express the excellence and quality of Danish handmade furniture. He worked fervently for the continuing improvement of the quality of Danish furniture and the expansion of the export markets, and he served as the president of the Cabinetmakers' Exhibition from 1952 to 1957. From 1944 to 1957 he served as president of the Arts and Crafts Committee for Export. He also served as vice president of the Danish Arts and Crafts National Association from 1940 to 1954. Jacob Kjær employed his talents and skills with extraordinary passion and dedication to his art and the industry that sustained it. His works grace the displays of several major art museums around the world.

HONORS> Hand Work Medal, 1954. Grand Prix from many international exhibitions.

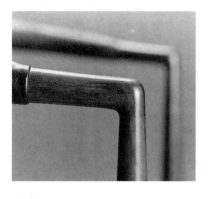

MATERIALS> Mahogany, Leather

24 x 22$^{13}/_{32}$ x 30$^{13}/_{32}$ / Sh 18$^{13}/_{16}$ in. / 15.4 lbs.

600 x 560 x 760 / Sh 470 mm / 7.0 kg

MANUFACTURER> Jacob Kjær, Christensen & Larsen Møbelhåndværk A/S

Produced for the United Nations Building in New York City, this representative example of Danish furniture, the F N Chair, is invariably included in books on the subject. Though its frame is rather slender, the chair itself is of a very strong construction yet remains elegant in form. The top rail is leather-bound wood, giving the chair warmth and comfort. Unfortunately, the chair is currently out of production.

DESIGNER(S)>	NAME>	YEAR>
JACOB KJÆR	F N CHAIR	1949

MATERIALS> Mahogany, Leather
24 x 22^{13}/$_{32}$ x 30^{13}/$_{32}$ / Sh 18^{19}/$_{32}$ in. / 19.8 lbs.
600 x 560 x 760 / Sh 465 mm / 9.0 kg
MANUFACTURER> Jacob Kjær, Christensen & Larsen
Møbelhåndværk A/S

This chair is an adaptation of the F N Chair.
The back of the seat is wider on this model,
making it more comfortable. The frame and
beam design is almost identical to those of the
F N Chair.

DESIGNER(S)>	NAME>	YEAR>
JACOB KJÆR	ARM CHAIR B-48	1950

MATERIALS> Teak, Leather or Teak, Cane
$22^{13}/_{32}$ x $21^{19}/_{32}$ x $32^{13}/_{16}$ / Sh $18^{13}/_{16}$ in. / 13.2 lbs.
560 x 540 x 820 / Sh 470 mm / 6.0 kg
MANUFACTURER> Jacob Kjær, Christensen & Larsen
Møbelhåndværk A/S

Though Jacob Kjær produced a great number of
works considered representative of the F N
Chair, he is primarily noted as being the owner
and snedkermaster (artist in charge of the
craftsmen making the furniture) of a studio specializing in the design and production of works
which are spectacular examples of Danish furniture. His exceptional talent and skill enabled
him to achieve designs marked by a harmonious
combination of function and beauty. This particular dining chair is an outstanding expression
of both beauty and simplicity.

Jacob Kjær / Dining chair / 1950 / Jacob Kjær, Christensen
& Larsen Møbelhåndværk A/S

MOGENS**KOCH**

[PROFESSOR, DESIGNER] **1898–1992**

MOGENS KOCH

Worked with Carl Petersen, 1921–25. Graduated from the Royal Danish Academy of Fine Arts, School of Architecture, 1925. Worked with Kaare Klint, 1925–30. Opened his own office in 1934. Professor of the Royal Danish Academy of Fine Arts, Building Design at the School of Architecture, 1950–68.

HONORS> Eckersberg Medal, 1938. C. F. Hansen Medal, 1963. Cabinetmakers' Guild annual prize, 1964. Honorary member of the Royal Danish Academy of Fine Arts, 1969. Danish Furniture Manufacturers Association's Furniture Prize, 1982. Danish Society of Design's ID Classic, 1990. Danmarks National Bank's Anniversary Foundation Prize, 1990.

MATERIALS> Teak, Fabric
26 x 26^{13}/$_{32}$ x 32^{13}/$_{32}$ / Sh 16^{3}/$_{16}$ in. / 30.36 lbs.
26 x 26 x 12/ Sh 16^{3}/$_{16}$ in. / 23.1 lbs.
650 x 660 x 810 / Sh 405 mm / 13.8 kg
650 x 650 x 300 / Sh 405 mm / 10.5 kg
MANUFACTURER> Rud. Rasmussens Snedkerier Aps.

The design for this chair was originally inspired
by the design for a similar sofa by Kaare Klint.
Klint's work was designed as an easy chair and
stool that combined to form a bed. In this
piece, a table is incorporated rather than a stool.
Unfortunately, the chair is no longer for sale.

DESIGNER(S)>	NAME>	YEAR>
MOGENS KOCH	ADDITIONS-SOFA	1933

MATERIALS> Beech, Canvas
21³/₁₆ x 20 x 32 / Sh 17¹³/₁₆ in. / 14.3 lbs.
530 x 500 x 800 / Sh 445 mm / 6.5 kg
MANUFACTURER> Interna, Rud. Rasmussens Snedkerier
Aps.

The design of this chair was originally based on
the design of a safari chair by Kaare Klint and
is now considered one of the most important
folding chairs in Danish furniture design. The
chair is familiar in Japan as a director's chair.
When it was first designed, it was considered
too radical to produce, but in 1960 Interna
finally put it into production. Since then, many
variations of this chair have been produced,
including children's chairs, tables, stools, and
a rack made specifically to go with this chair.

DESIGNER(S)>	NAME>	YEAR>
MOGENS KOCH	FOLDING CHAIR	1932, PRODUCED 1960

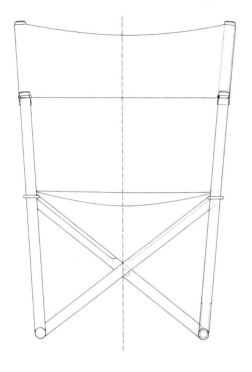

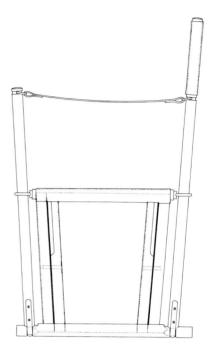

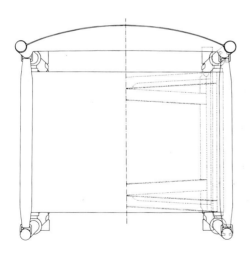

MATERIALS> Mahogany, Leather
25¹⁹/₃₂ x 35¹³/₃₂ x 48 / Sh 17¹³/₃₂ in. / 51.7 lbs.
24 x 23³/₁₆ x 13¹/₂ / Sh 13⁵/₁₆ in. / 13.4 lbs.
640 x 885 x 1200 / Sh 435 mm / 23.5 kg
600 x 580 x 340 / Sh 332 mm / 6.1 kg
MANUFACTURER> Prototype was made by Holger Larsen, Interna, Rud. Rasmussens Snedkerier Aps.

Kaare Klint produced many redesigns of eighteenth-century English furniture. These designs were later simplified by Mogens Koch, who added his own ideas and altered them again. This wingback chair includes many features that are not found in English furniture, including a double cushion, one of which can be used on the stool. In addition, the seat of the chair is not fixed to the legs but is instead merely placed on top. Interna began production of these chairs in 1964.

| DESIGNER(S)> | NAME> | YEAR> |
| MOGENS KOCH | WINGBACK CHAIR | 1936, PRODUCED 1964 |

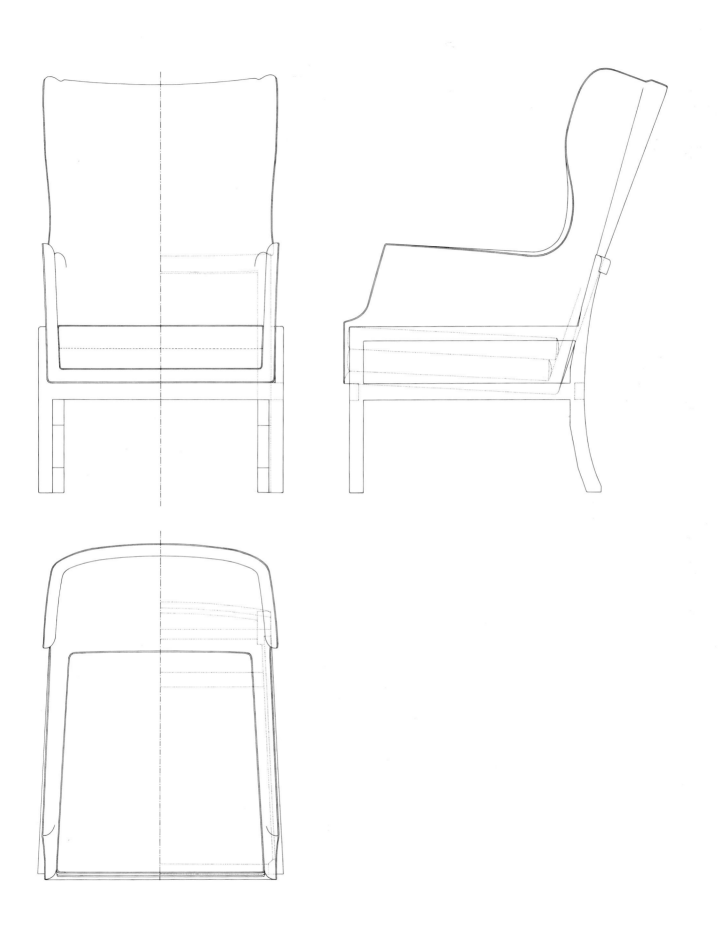

FRITZ**HENNINGSEN**

[SNEDKERMASTER] **DATE OF BIRTH AND DEATH UNKNOWN**

FRITZ HENNINGSEN

Fritz Henningsen was both a furniture workshop owner and a designer. There is very little information available about him, but he is believed to have been born sometime before 1900. He has been an active member of the Cabinetmakers' Guild since 1927. This rocking chair shows some traditional features. Its beautiful curves provide an elegant atmosphere and are the chair's most outstanding feature.

MATERIALS> Teak, Leather
27 x 30 x 34³/₁₆ / Sh 17¹⁹/₃₂ in. / 34.32 lbs.
675 x 750 x 855 / Sh 440 mm / 15.6 kg
MANUFACTURER> Fritz Henningsen

Fritz Henningsen / Easy chair / c. 1930 / Fritz Henningsen

DESIGNER(S)>	NAME>	YEAR>
FRITZ HENNINGSEN	ROCKING CHAIR	1930

MATERIALS> Mahogany, Fabric
26¹³/₁₆ x 28 x 36¹³/₃₂ / Sh 18.32 in. / 44.22 lbs.
670 x 700 x 910 / Sh 458 mm / 20.1 kg
MANUFACTURER> Fritz Henningsen

This chair was exhibited at the Tenth Cabinetmakers' Guild Exhibition held at the Arts and Crafts Museum in Copenhagen in 1936. The designer of this chair participated in the Cabinetmakers' Guild Exhibition for ten years and this chair concluded his contribution to the event. Horsehair and cotton, the most popular materials of the time for this purpose, were used for the cushions. The simplicity of the chair's design demonstrates the designer's appreciation for traditional styles.

DESIGNER(S)>	NAME>	YEAR>
FRITZ HENNINGSEN	EASY CHAIR	1936

EDVARD**KINDT-LARSEN**

[ARCHITECT] **1901–82**

TOVE**KINDT-LARSEN**

[ARCHITECT] **1906–**

EDVARD KINDT-LARSEN

Edvard Kindt-Larsen graduated from the School of Building Technology in 1922 and in 1927 from the Royal Danish Academy of Fine Arts, School of Architecture. From 1945 to 1953, he served as principal of the School of Arts, Crafts, and Design. In 1937, he opened an architecture office with Tove Kindt-Larsen.

HONORS> Academy's Gold Medal, 1931. First prize, Cabinetmakers' Guild furniture competition, 1938, 1940, 1941, and 1943. Second prize, A. Michelsen anniversary competition, 1940. First prize amber design competition, 1943. Cabinetmakers' Guild annual prize, 1951. Awards from many other competitions.

TOVE KINDT-LARSEN

Tove Kindt-Larsen studied at the Royal Danish Academy of Fine Arts, School of Architecture. Opened architecture office with Edvard Kindt-Larsen in 1937.

HONORS> Cabinetmakers' Guild annual prize, 1957. Gold medal for textiles, California State Fair and Exposition, 1956, 1958, 1960, and 1961. Many prizes and awards in collaboration with Edvard Kindt-Larsen.

MATERIALS> Oak, Leather
27 x 30³/₁₆ x 32 / Sh 12³/₁₆ in. / 33 lbs.
675 x 755 x 800 / Sh 306 mm / 15.0 kg
MANUFACTURER> Gustav Bertelsen & Co. (Kund Jensen)

One of the important Danish chair designs of the 1930s. Meant for use in front of a fireplace, this masterpiece combined the talents of Edvard Kindt-Larsen and Tove Kindt-Larsen. The chair is distinguished by the X-shaped crossbar under the seat and the shape of the arm top. The seat and seat back are designed as one piece; a stool for this chair was designed simultaneously.

DESIGNER(S)>	NAME>	YEAR>
EDVARD KINDT-LARSEN / TOVE KINDT-LARSEN	FIREPLACE CHAIR	1939

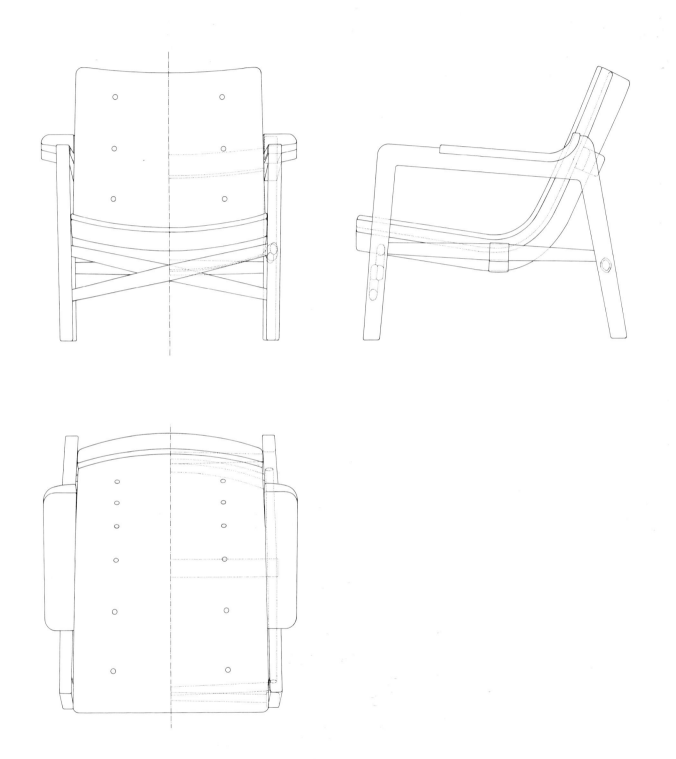

FIREPLACE CHAIR

MATERIALS> Beech, Teak, Fabric
27^{13}/$_{32}$ x 32 x 32^3/$_{16}$ / Sh 16^{13}/$_{32}$ in. / 26.84 lbs.
685 x 800 x 805 / Sh 410 mm / 12.2 kg
MANUFACTURER> France & Søn

Originally France & Søn textiles, this company started to make furniture in the early 1950s. Such well-known designers as Finn Juhl, Ole Wanscher, and Grete Jalk worked for the company. Then Kindt-Larsen made this easy chair design for France & Søn, which was awarded a prize at the Milano Triennale. Its form is similar to No. 17.

| DESIGNER(S)> | NAME> | YEAR> |
| EDVARD KINDT-LARSEN / TOVE KINDT-LARSEN | EASY CHAIR № 116 | 1954 |

MATERIALS> Mahogany, Fabric
88 x 31 x 34¹³/₃₂ / Sh 13¹⁹/₃₂ in. / 72.6 lbs.
2200 x 775 x 860 / Sh 340 mm / 33.0 kg
MANUFACTURER> Thorald Madsen's Snedkeri

The most interesting element of this sofa is its legs, which exhibit a truss construction. The body shape is wider at the seat, which gives a feeling of size.

DESIGNER(S)>
EDVARD KINDT-LARSEN / TOVE KINDT-LARSEN

NAME>
SOFA

YEAR>
1956

MATERIALS> Rosewood, Leather
16⁷/₈ x 16⁷/₈ x 17³¹/₃₂ / Sh 17³¹/₃₂ in. / 9.9 lbs.
422 x 422 x 449 / Sh 449 mm / 4.5 kg
MANUFACTURER> Thorald Madsen's Snedkeri, A. J.
Iversen

This stool, made of luxurious, extremely rare
Brazilian rosewood, is a good example of the
use of superior materials for excellent designs.

DESIGNER(S)>
EDVARD KINDT-LARSEN / TOVE KINDT-LARSEN

NAME>
STOOL

YEAR>
1957

FLEMMING**LASSEN**

[ARCHITECT] **1902–84**

FLEMMING LASSEN

Flemming Lassen studied at the school of bricklayer technology in Copenhagen and studied with architect Th.Hjejle. Niels Rosenkjær. He worked with Arne Jacobsen and opened his own office in 1939.

HONORS> Eckersberg Medal, 1940. Gentofte Municipality Prize, 1941 and 1957. Frederiksberg Municipality Prize, 1943.

MATERIALS> Mahogany, Cane
20 x 18^{13}/$_{32}$ x 33^{3}/$_{16}$ / Sh 18^{3}/$_{16}$ in. / 8.8 lbs.
500 x 460 x 830 / Sh 455 mm / 4.0 kg
MANUFACTURER> A. J. Iversen

This dining chair is one of a series of chairs (including an arm chair) designed by Flemming Lassen. The seat and back have been accented by making them of woven cane. At the time they were designed, the arm chair was considered radical but the dining chair was seen as a simpler design.

DESIGNER(S)> FLEMMING LASSEN	NAME> DINING CHAIR	YEAR> 1955

MOGENS**LASSEN**

[ARCHITECT] 1901–87

MOGENS LASSEN

Mogens Lassen studied at the school of architecture technology in Copenhagen from 1919 to 1923. Studied with Edvard Heiberg, Tyge Hvass, and Ole Falkentorp. Opened his own office in 1932.

HONORS> Danish Architects honorary medal, 1971. C. F. Hansen Medal, 1971.

MATERIALS> Steel pipe, Leather
20 x 18^{19}/$_{32}$ x 25^{19}/$_{32}$ / Sh 16^{13}/$_{16}$ in. / 13.2 lbs.
500 x 465 x 640 / Sh 420 mm / 6.0 kg
MANUFACTURER> Fritz Hansens Eftf.

The German (Weimar) Bauhaus school of design influenced furniture design in many European countries. Though Kaare Klint exercised a great deal of influence in the world of Danish furniture design, the presence of the Bauhaus influence was also felt. This design, created by Mogens Lassen, was originally taken from the steel pipe furniture designs of Mies van der Rohe and Marcel Bruer. It is one of the earliest Danish steel pipe chair or stool designs.

DESIGNER(S)>	NAME>	YEAR>
MOGENS LASSEN	ARM STOOL	1930

MATERIALS> Teak
$19^3/_{16}$ x $14^{13}/_{32}$ x $20^3/_{16}$ / Sh $20^3/_{16}$ in. / 7.92 lbs.
480 x 360 x 505 / Sh 505 mm / 3.6 kg
MANUFACTURER> K. Thomsen

Three-legged stools are a popular item of agricultural furniture of northern Europe. These
stools are characterized by their enhancement
of the natural wood from which they are made
and for the rough simplicity of the craftsmanship. Their forms, as exemplified by these striking stools designed by Mogens Lassen, convey
a feeling of warmth and presence. The legs are
screw-on, knockdown construction.

DESIGNER(S)>
MOGENS LASSEN

NAME>
STOOL

YEAR>
1942

ARNE**JACOBSEN**
[ARCHITECT, DESIGNER] **1902–71**

ARNE JACOBSEN

Arne Jacobsen graduated from the Royal Danish Academy of Fine Arts, School of Architectural Design in 1927. After graduation, he produced many designs that were to characterize modern Danish architecture and establish the concept of architectural functionalism. During this period he was also active as a furniture designer and created many excellent pieces. He was especially known for his employment of new techniques and materials in his work and for creating new horizons for the world of Danish design through the mass production of these pieces. As an architect, he dedicated himself not only to the design of the buildings themselves, but also to the overall harmony of the structure with its environment. His designs cover a wide range of works, from daily utensils to interior fabrics to exterior gardens. No other designer has ever been able to maintain such prolific activity or such scope. He served as a professor at the Royal Danish Academy of Fine Arts from 1956 to 1965.

HONORS> Silver medal, World Exposition in Paris, 1925. Small gold medal of the Royal Danish Academy of Fine Arts, 1926. Eckersberg Medal, 1936. C. F. Hansen Medal, 1955. Grand prize and silver medal, Milano Triennale, 1957. Grand Prix International d'Architecture, 1962. Federation of Danish Architects honorary medal, 1962. Ph.D. from Causus, Oxford University, 1966. ID Prize, 1967, 1969.

MATERIALS> Oak, Leather
20³/₁₆ x 21¹³/₁₆ x 34 / Sh 17 in. / 9.9 lbs.
505 x 545 x 850 / Sh 425 mm / 4.5 kg
MANUFACTURER> Fritz Hansens Eftf.

This chair is one of Jacobsen's early works. It was designed to be included in a restaurant constructed in Klampenborg designed by Jacobsen. The chair's design suggests a strong influence from Chinese chairs from the Ming Dynasty. Although the chair was made by Fritz Hansens Co., it was never mass-produced for sale.

| DESIGNER(S)> | NAME> | YEAR> |
| ARNE JACOBSEN | DINING CHAIR | 1935 |

MATERIALS> Oak, Fabric
23^{13}/$_{16}$ x 21^{13}/$_{32}$ x 34^{19}/$_{32}$ / Sh 19^{13}/$_{32}$ in. / 15.4 lbs.
595 x 535 x 865 / Sh 485 mm / 7.0 kg
MANUFACTURER> maker unknown

The Åuhus City Hall is a representative example of Jacobsen's early architectural work and was designed in collaboration with Erik Møller. At the time, Hans J. Wegner (who was still unknown) designed furniture for the project as an employee of Jacobsen. Though this chair was designed for the city hall, Wegner produced many similar works during the same period.

DESIGNER(S)>	NAME>	YEAR>
ARNE JACOBSEN / ERIK MØLLER	ARM CHAIR	1937–42

MATERIALS> Molded polyurethane, Steel, Fabric
28 $^{13}/_{16}$ x 24$^{13}/_{32}$ x 28 / Sh 16 in. / 14.3 lbs.
720 x 610 x 700 / Sh 400 mm / 6.5 kg
MANUFACTURER> Fritz Hansens Eftf.

Unique and interesting names, based on their forms, distinguish Jacobsen's works and have become well known. This chair is called the Pot Chair, a name well suited to its distinctive shape. This chair and another almost exactly like it created by a company in France were unveiled in the same year. Influenced by the Egg Chair and the Swan Chair, the seat totally envelops a person's body.

MATERIALS> Beech, Steel
$20^{13}/_{32}$ x $20^{13}/_{32}$ x $30^{13}/_{16}$ / Sh $17^{19}/_{32}$ in. / 6.93 lbs.
510 x 510 x 770 / Sh 440 mm / 3.15 kg
MANUFACTURER> Fritz Hansens Eftf.

Created for use in the dining room of the Novo Pharmaceutical Company, this chair takes its name from the shape of the body, which resembles an ant. The chair was originally designed with three legs, though later models were made with four legs for greater stability.

| DESIGNER(S)> | NAME> | | YEAR> |
| ARNE JACOBSEN | THE ANT CHAIR Nº 3100 | | 1951 |

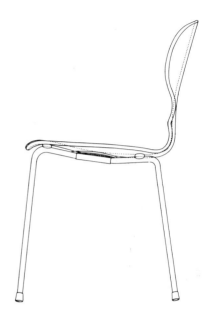

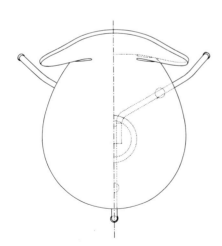

THE ANT CHAIR   Nº 3100

MATERIALS> Teak
$19^3/_{16}$ x $20^{13}/_{32}$ x $3^3/_{16}$ / Sh 17 in. / 6.16 lbs.
480 x 510 x 780 / Sh 425 mm / 2.8 kg
MANUFACTURER> Fritz Hansens Eftf.

The seat and legs of this chair are made of laminated wood and the shape of the back is more angular than the Ant Chair. The deeper curve of the seat provides comfort. Note the hexagonal cross-section of the legs.

DESIGNER(S)>	NAME>	YEAR>
ARNE JACOBSEN	LAMINATED CHAIR Nº 4130	1955

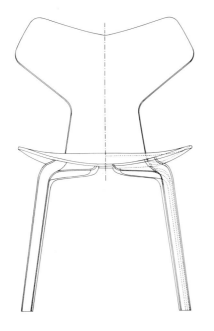
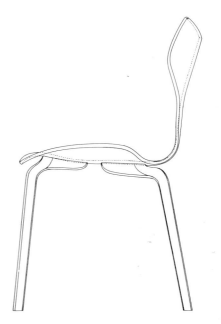
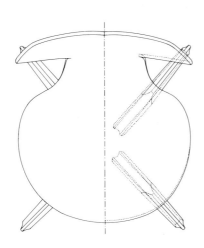

MATERIALS> Molded polyurethane, Cast aluminum, Leather

$34^{13}/_{32}$ x $31^{19}/_{32}$ x $42^{13}/_{16}$ / Sh $13^{19}/_{32}$ in. / 42.46 lbs.
$22^{13}/_{32}$ x $16^{13}/_{32}$ x $17^{19}/_{32}$ / Sh $15^{3}/_{16}$ in. / 11 lbs.
860 x 790 x 1070 / Sh 340 mm / 19.3 kg
560 x 410 x 440 / Sh 380 mm / 5.0 kg
MANUFACTURER> Fritz Hansens Eftf.

Designed for use in the lobby of the SAS Royal Hotel in Copenhagen, the seat, back, and arms of this chair are formed of a single piece of molded polyurethane. Arne Jacobsen's unique use of polyurethane for furniture design and the chair's construction became the talk of the industry. Sitting in the chair at a slight reclining angle, enveloped by its shape, proves to be a comfortable experience.

| DESIGNER(S)> | NAME> | | | YEAR> |
| ARNE JACOBSEN | THE EGG CHAIR Nº 3317 | STOOL Nº 3127 | | 1958 |

MATERIALS> Molded polyurethane, Steel, Leather
18¹³/₃₂ x 21¹⁹/₃₂ x 35¹⁹/₃₂ / Sh 18¹³/₃₂ in. / 13.2 lbs.
460 x 540 x 890 / Sh 460 mm / 6.0 kg
MANUFACTURER> Fritz Hansens Eftf.

Not nearly as well known as the Egg Chair, the
Drop Chair was used as a bar chair in the SAS
Royal Hotel in Copenhagen. As with the Egg
Chair, the seat and back of the Drop Chair are
molded polyurethane. Today, one suite in the
SAS Royal Hotel has been restored as originally
designed by Jacobsen. In that room, which is
still used for guests, the furnishings of 1958
are displayed, including the chairs.

DESIGNER(S)>	NAME>	YEAR>
ARNE JACOBSEN	THE DROP CHAIR	1958

MATERIALS> Molded polyurethane, Cast aluminum, Fabric
$29^{19}/_{32}$ x $27^3/_{16}$ x 30 / Sh $15^3/_{16}$ in. / 22 lbs.
740 x 680 x 750 / Sh 380 mm / 10.0 kg
MANUFACTURER> Fritz Hansens Eftf.

The Swan Chair was named for its form, which resembles a swan spreading its wings. The seat of the chair is made of the same material as the Egg Chair. An early one-fifth scale model of the design shows the chair with legs of thin, steel pipes. The first full-scale model had four legs made of laminated wood. Later, the chair was produced with the same leg design as the Egg Chair. Another version of the chair was a sofa that could accommodate two people. The Swan Chair can be seen in the lobby of the SAS Royal Hotel.

DESIGNER(S)>	NAME>		YEAR>
ARNE JACOBSEN	SWAN CHAIR	Nº 3320	1958

MATERIALS> Molded polyurethane, Beech
24 x 22³/₁₆ x 41¹³/₃₂ / Sh 17¹⁹/₃₂ in. / 14.3 lbs.
600 x 555 x 1035 / Sh 440 mm / 6.5 kg
MANUFACTURER> Fritz Hansens Eftf.

This extremely rare piece was designed for use
in the dining room of the SAS Royal Hotel. Just
as with the Drop Chair, the piece was never put
into mass production. The body is molded
polyurethane and the frame and legs are laminated wood.

| DESIGNER(S)> | NAME> | YEAR> |
| ARNE JACOBSEN | DINING CHAIR | 1958 |

MATERIALS> Beech, Steel
24¹³/₁₆ x 20¹³/₁₆ x 31¹⁹/₃₂ / Sh 17¹⁹/₃₂ in. / 11.22 lbs.
620 x 520 x 790 / Sh 440 mm / 5.1 kg
MANUFACTURER> Fritz Hansens Eftf.

A representative work of the designer, this chair is well-known all over the world. Variations of this model have been produced, some with casters, some with a small writing arm, and some with hooks for joining them together. The variations were created to fulfill specific needs. Together with an oval table designed by Piet Hein, these chairs were sold as dining chairs by Fritz Hansens.

Arne Jacobsen / Arm chair / 1970 / Fritz Hansens Eftf.

DESIGNER(S)>	NAME>	YEAR>
ARNE JACOBSEN	SEVEN CHAIR № 3107	1955

MAGNUS**STEPHENSEN**

[ARCHITECT, DESIGNER] **1903–84**

MAGNUS STEPHENSEN

Magnus Stephensen graduated from the school of technology in 1924 and from the Royal Danish Academy of Fine Arts, School of Architecture in 1931. He opened his own office in 1932.

HONORS> Eckersberg Medal, 1948. Milano Triennale, Gold Medal, 1951 and 1957. Grand Prix twice, 1954. Silver Medal, 1960. Honorary Member of Industrial Designers, Denmark 1971.

MATERIALS> Beech, Fabric
$16^{13}/_{32}$ x 20 x $31^{3}/_{16}$ / Sh $19^{19}/_{32}$ in. / 11 lbs.
410 x 500 x 780 / Sh 490 mm / 5.0 kg
MANUFACTURER> Fritz Hansens Eftf.

Around 1930, Fritz Hansens produced the bentwood furniture of Austrian designer Michael Thonet. This chair shows the influence of the Thonet designs. At that time, many bentwood chairs were made of beech.

DESIGNER(S)>	NAME>	YEAR>
MAGNUS STEPHENSEN	DINING CHAIR	CA. 1930

OLE**WANSCHER**
[PROFESSOR, DESIGNER] **1903–85**

OLE WANSCHER

Ole Wanscher studied under Kaare Klint at the Royal Danish Academy of Fine Arts and graduated from the Academy in 1929. He succeeded Klint in 1955 and served as a professor in the Department of Furniture Design at the Academy. The influence of his father, a scholar in the field of history of fine arts, sparked his interest in the history of furniture design, leading him to Egypt and several European countries for research. His work in this field resulted in the publication of a number of books and papers. He was particularly fond of Egyptian, Greek, Chinese, and eighteenth-century English furniture and is well known for his adoption of the beautiful lines and forms of these classical styles. Most of his works have been created from natural materials, and the fabrics employed for binding are natural color combinations, making use of materials such as black leather and woven horsehair. His works, however, were not designed only for the elite. He was one of the first designers to create works for mass production, and these pieces were designed for functionality and convenience.
HONORS> Milano Triennale Grand Prix, 1960. Copenhagen Cabinetmakers' annual prize, 1960.

MATERIALS> Rosewood, Cane, Leather
26 x 26¹³/₃₂ x 34 / Sh 16 in. / 20.24 lbs.
650 x 660 x 850 / Sh 400 mm / 9.2 kg
MANUFACTURER> P. Jeppesen

The elegant simplicity of this chair shows Wanscher at his best. The back is similar to that of English ladder-back chairs built in the 1750s and 1760s. The seat is made of woven cane, and its cushion of leather is filled with feathers. In addition to this easy chair, a dining chair was designed. Most of the furniture currently produced by P. Jeppesen is designed by Wanscher. Virtually all of Wanscher's designs are elegant works finished to a high level of perfection.

DESIGNER(S)>
OLE WANSCHER

NAME>
EASY CHAIR № 149

YEAR>
1949

MATERIALS> Oak, Cane
26³/₁₆ x 28¹³/₁₆ x 30¹³/₁₆ / Sh 14¹³/₁₆ in. / 19.8 lbs.
655 x 720 x 770 / Sh 370 mm / 9.0 kg
MANUFACTURER> Rud. Rasmussens Snedkerier Aps.

This chair was shown at the Cabinetmakers' Guild Exhibition in 1951. It was the first piece by Wanscher made in cooperation with Rud Rasmussens. The distinguishing feature of this chair are the arms resembling animals' horns. These beautiful arms set the piece apart from the works of Finn Juhl and Hans J. Wegner. The details of its design, such as the joining of arms and legs, show a high mastery of furniture making techniques. The seat pictured is rattan; the chair was also made in an upholstered-cloth version.

DESIGNER(S)> OLE WANSCHER   NAME> EASY CHAIR   YEAR> 1951

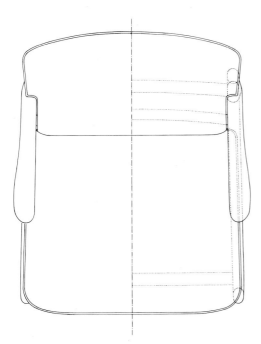

MATERIALS> Mahogany, Leather
26^{19}/$_{32}$ x 32^{13}/$_{32}$ x 38 / Sh 16^{13}/$_{32}$ in. / 28.16 lbs.
665 x 810 x 950 / Sh 410 mm / 12.8 kg
MANUFACTURER> France & Søn

France & Søn, the factory that designed this chair, specializes in mass-produced, machine-made furniture rather than hand-crafted pieces. Even so, these machine-produced pieces exhibit the warmth usually seen in handmade furniture and are representative of the Danish tradition of fine furniture. The knockdown construction of the rocking chair allows the seat and frame to be taken apart to facilitate transport. The comfortable, organic curves of the arms and back demonstrate the extent to which this chair was designed to accommodate the human body.

Ole Wanscher / Rocking chair / ca. 1951 / France & Søn

DESIGNER(S)> OLE WANSCHER | NAME> ROCKING CHAIR | YEAR> 1951

MATERIALS> Rosewood, Leather
25 x 22 x 31^{19}/$_{32}$ / Sh 18^{3}/$_{16}$ in. / 19.8 lbs.
625 x 550 x 790 / Sh 455 mm / 9.0 kg
MANUFACTURER> A. J. Iversen

There are three variations of this arm chair; the
other variations have top rails upholstered with
leather for an extremely soft, comfortable contact with the back. The top rail is simply joined
in the center. It is interesting to see Wanscher's
treatment of Hans Wegner's design of the top
rail of the chair.

Ole Wanscher / Arm chair / ca. 1958 / A. J. Iversen

Ole Wanscher / Arm chair / ca. 1958 / A. J. Iversen

DESIGNER(S)>
OLE WANSCHER

NAME>
ARM CHAIR

YEAR>
1958

MATERIALS> Mahogany, Sheepskin
22 x 12 (6⁹/₃₂) x 16¹³/₁₆ / Sh 16 (19¹⁹/₃₂) in. / 4.4 lbs.
550 x 300 (157) x 420 / Sh 400 (490) mm / 2.0 kg
MANUFACTURER> A. J. Iversen

The design of this chair is based on an ancient Egyptian stool now in the collection of the Staatliche Museum in Berlin. The original stool was excavated in 1934. The frame of this work is almost the same shape as the original piece. This three-thousand-year-old form seems astonishingly modern.

DESIGNER(S)>
OLE WANSCHER
NAME>
EGYPTIAN STOOL
YEAR>
1960

72

MATERIALS> Rosewood, Horsehair
$25^{3}/_{16}$ x $22^{19}/_{32}$ x 32 / Sh $18^{19}/_{32}$ in. / 14.3 lbs.
630 x 565 x 800 / Sh 465 mm / 6.5 kg
MANUFACTURER> A. J. Iversen

An excellent example of a work as created by a master designer, this piece was made of the very best materials by the expert craftsman Iversen. The frame is Brazilian rosewood, a rare wood that is difficult to obtain. The seat is woven horsehair, a durable material that is said to withstand one hundred years of use. Extravagant and elegant, this work is a masterpiece of quality and design. Another chair with armrests was also produced.

Ole Wanscher / Dining chair / 1962 / A. J. Iversen

DESIGNER(S)>	NAME>	YEAR>
OLE WANSCHER	ARM CHAIR	1962

MATERIALS> Rosewood, Leather
20 x 19¹³/₁₆ x 35 / Sh 17³/₁₆ in. / 13.64 lbs.
500 x 495 x 875 / Sh 430 mm / 6.2 kg
MANUFACTURER> A. J. Iversen

Originally designed by Wanscher in 1940, this chair was shown at the Cabinetmakers' Guild Exhibition the same year. The model shown here is a 1963 redesigned version referred to as Benedikte. Whether the origin of the name was the hero of Shakespeare's famous comedy or the saint gracing the walls of churches is not known.

DESIGNER(S)>
OLE WANSCHER

NAME>
BENEDIKTE DINING CHAIR

YEAR>
1963

SØREN**HANSEN**

[DESIGNER] **1905–77**

SØREN HANSEN

Journeyman joiner, 1925. Studied in Denmark, Sweden, and France. Employed by Fritz Hansens Co., 1928. Joint operator since 1933 and director from 1955–77. Chairman of Danish Crafts Council from 1951–58.

MATERIALS> Beech
28 x 24^{13}/$_{32}$ x 29^{3}/$_{16}$ / Sh 15^{3}/$_{16}$ in. / 13.2 lbs.
700 x 610 x 740 / Sh 380 mm / 6.0 kg
MANUFACTURER> Fritz Hansens Eftf.

The seat and back are made of laminated wood and the frame of bentwood. The design shows the influence of Thonet. A two-person chair of the same design dates from this period.

DESIGNER(S)>	NAME>	YEAR>
SØREN HANSEN	EASY CHAIR	CA. 1941

PIET**HEIN**

[DESIGNER] **1905–96**

PIET HEIN

Studied at the Royal Swedish Academy of Fine
Arts, 1942. Studied natural science at
Copenhagen University.

HONORS> Honorary Doctorate, Yale University,
1972. Honorary Craftsman of Copenhagen,
1975. The Alexander Graham Bell Silver Bell,
1968. ID prize, 1971. Die Gute Industreform,
1971.

MATERIALS> Steel, Leather
$14^{19}/_{32}$ x $14^{19}/_{32}$ x $32^{13}/_{32}$ / Sh $32^{19}/_{32}$ in. / 20.68 lbs.
365 x 365 x 810 / Sh 815 mm / 9.4 kg
MANUFACTURER> Fritz Hansens Eftf.

Known as a philosopher, game designer, and
poet as well as furniture designer, the multi-
talented Piet Hein devised a formula for a super
ellipse that he used for the shape of table tops.
This stool has legs constructed on the same
principle as the legs of elliptical tables.

DESIGNER(S)>	NAME>	YEAR>
PIET HEIN	BAR STOOL	1961

MOGENS**VOLTELEN**

[ARCHITECT] **1908–95**

MOGENS VOLTELEN

Graduated from the Royal Danish Academy of Fine Arts. Worked with Poul Henningsen and Vilhelm Lauritzen. Opened his own office in 1928. Teacher of Architecture at the Royal Danish Academy of Fine Art, 1940; assistant professor, 1959–78.

HONORS> PH Prize, 1969. Grant from Danish State Art Foundation, 1979.

MATERIALS> Mahogany, Leather
$24^{13}/_{16}$ x $34^{3}/_{16}$ x $38^{13}/_{32}$ / Sh $13^{13}/_{16}$ in. / 24.86 lbs.
620 x 855 x 960 / Sh 345 mm / 11.3 kg
MANUFACTURER> Niels Vodder

This chair is at first glance reminiscent of a Spanish folk chair design. The frame that extends to become the back legs of the chair makes the chair comfortable for sitting. Niels Vodder, the man who produced this chair, often worked in association with Finn Juhl. Mogens Voltelen, the designer of this chair, was responsible for inducing these two men to work together, a cooperative arrangement that gained worldwide acclaim.

ORLAMØLGAARDNIELSEN

[ARCHITECT, DESIGNER] **1907–94**

PETERHVIDT

[DESIGNER] **1916–86**

ORLA MØLGAARD NIELSEN

Served his apprenticeship at the Nielsen Brothers in Iborg. Completed craftsman school at the Museum of Industrial Art. Attended the Department of Furnishing and Interior Design at the Art Academy in Copenhagen. Employed by architects Kaare Klint, Helweg Møller, Arne Jacobsen, and Palle Suenson. Founded and operated a design company from 1944–75 (together with Peter Hvidt and from 1970 with Hans Kristensen). Teacher at the School of Fine Art and Craft, 1936–45. Aesthetic adviser for the construction of the Bridge of Lilleb It (Little Belt) and highways in the counties of Roskilde and Hoblk.

HONORS> Diploma of Honor at Milano Triennale, 1951 and 1954.

PETER HVIDT

Graduated from the School of Arts, Crafts, and Design, 1940. Opened office with Orla Mølgaard Nielsen from 1944 to 1975 and with Hans Kristensen since 1970.

HONORS> Prizes in furniture and industrial design competitions. Diploma of Honor at Milano Triennale, 1951 and 1954.

MATERIALS> Teak
24 x 20¹³/₁₆ x 32¹⁹/₃₂ / Sh 17¹³/₃₂ in. / 12.76 lbs.
600 x 520 x 815 / Sh 435 mm / 5.8 kg
MANUFACTURER> Portex

One of the oldest Danish examples of the stacking chair. A similar chair was designed by the Swedish architect Erik Gunnar Asplund between 1935 and 1937. A model with an upholstered seat and back and an armless chair were designed about the same time.

DESIGNER(S)>
ORLA MØLGAARD NIELSEN / PETER HVIDT

NAME>
PORTEX STACKING CHAIR

YEAR>
1944

78

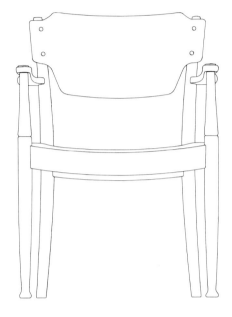

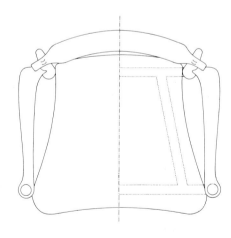

PORTEX STACKING CHAIR

MATERIALS> Teak, Beech
24^{13}/$_{16}$ x 28^{13}/$_{32}$ x 30^{13}/$_{32}$ / Sh 16 in. / 13.64 lbs.
620 x 710 x 760 / Sh 400 mm / 6.2 kg
MANUFACTURER> Fritz Hansens Eftf.

An adaptation for mass production of the AX Chair designed in 1947. The seat and back are laminated wood. This knockdown AX chair series was designed for ease and low cost of transportation and was one of the best-selling chairs internationally in the 1950s. A one-armed chair and an armless chair were designed at the same time.

Orla M. Nielsen, Peter Hvidt / AX chair / 1950 / Fritz Hansens Eftf.

Orla M. Nielsen, Peter Hvidt / AX chair / 1947 / Fritz Hansens Eftf.

DESIGNER(S)>	NAME>	YEAR>
ORLA MØLGAARD NIELSEN / PETER HVIDT	AX CHAIR № 6020	1950

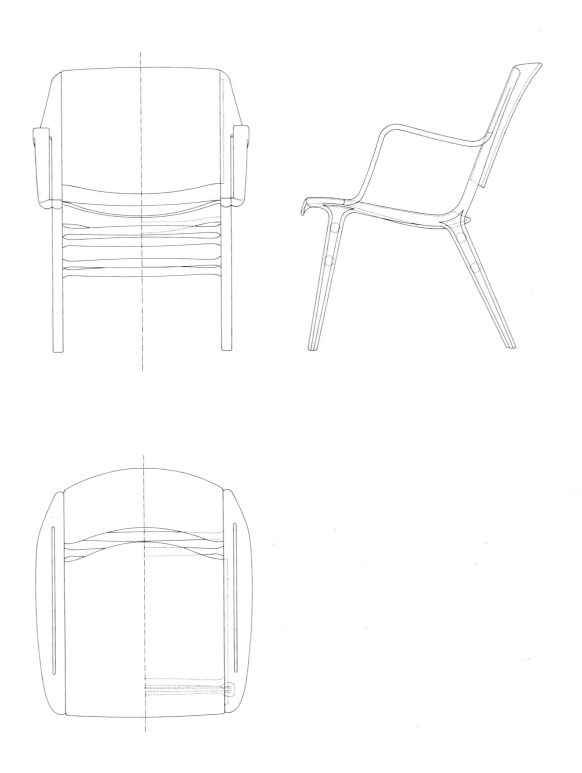

NAME>

AX CHAIR Nº 6020

MATERIALS> Beech, Teak, Fabric
25¹³/₁₆ x 30 x 33³/₁₆ / Sh 17¹⁹/₃₂ in. / 29.7 lbs.
645 x 750 x 830 / Sh 440 mm / 13.5 kg
MANUFACTURER> France & Søn

This chair was designed by France & Søn for mass production. Its distinguishing feature is the beautiful curved arm of laminated wood. Dark teak was used on the surface of the arms to protect them from stains and lighter beech was used underneath. The same layering technique was used on the legs as well.

DESIGNER(S)>
ORLA MØLGAARD NIELSEN / PETER HVIDT

NAME>
EASY CHAIR

YEAR>
CA. 1953

MATERIALS> Teak, Papercord

$24^{3}/_{16}$ x $20^{13}/_{16}$ x $31^{3}/_{16}$ / Sh 17.32 in. / 12.1 lbs.

605 x 520 x 780 / Sh 433 mm / 5.5 kg

MANUFACTURER> Søborg Møbelfabrik

This chair's seat is constructed of two pieces of laminated wood to form a comfortable curve for the human body. Details such as the bars under the seat and the shape of the arms show strong influence by the designs of Finn Juhl.

Orla M. Nielsen, Peter Hvidt / Dining chair / ca. 1956 / Søborg Møbelfabrik

DESIGNER(S)>
ORLA MØLGAARD NIELSEN / PETER HVIDT

NAME>
ARM CHAIR

YEAR>
CA. 1956

FINN**JUHL**

[ARCHITECT, DESIGNER] **1912–89**

FINN JUHL

Finn Juhl studied under Professor Kay Fisker at the Royal Danish Academy of Fine Arts. He graduated from the Academy in 1934. The main current of Danish design was created by a student of Kaare Klint, but Finn Juhl created a new, totally different approach characterized by new expressions of form and ideas. He worked with Vilherm Lauritzen in his architectural design office and at the same time designed many excellent works in cooperation with cabinetmaker Niels Vodder. His works are characterized by a unique feeling of sculptured beauty and singular perceptions of form in what was to become an individual style of design. He is ranked with the most famous of Danish designers. A stability of construction harmonized with a unique expression of form distinguish his works. This overall balance is particularly evident in his masterpiece, the Chieftain's Chair. His fondness for teak as a material led him to develop new and superior techniques for its employment, and he is responsible for the present popularity of teak in Danish furniture. In 1945, he became an independent architect and designer and served as the senior instructor at the School of Interior Design. While there he taught and influenced many budding designers who went on to become well known in their own rights. Because of his attention to detail, he is known as the sculptor of furniture design.

HONORS> C. F. Hansen incentive prize, 1944. Eckersberg Medal, 1947. Honorary diploma and gold medals at the Milano Triennale, 1957 and 1964. Honorary Royal Designer of Industry, London, 1978.

MATERIALS> Maple, Fabric
$34^{13}/_{16}$ x $31^{3}/_{16}$ x $28^{13}/_{16}$ / Sh 15.2 in. / 60.5 lbs.
870 x 780 x 720 / Sh 380 mm / 27.5 kg
MANUFACTURER> Niels Vodder

Finn Juhl first trained as an architect and later designed furniture, tableware, lamps and other works. His furniture designs differed markedly from those of the Klint school. After gaining international recognition, his reputation was established in Denmark. This design is from his early years. The chair was named for its resemblance to the shape of a pelican with outspread wings.

MATERIALS> Mahogany, Fabric
27^{19}/$_{32}$ x 31^{3}/$_{16}$ x 33 / Sh 14^{13}/$_{16}$ in.
690 x 780 x 825 / Sh 370 mm
MANUFACTURER> Niels Vodder, Søren Horn, Niels
Roth Andersen

The arms of this chair have been called the
most beautiful in the world. They are sharp-
edged like a paper knife and have a stunning
three-dimensional curve. The chair demonstrates a major change in Juhl's concept of
design. His early works had heavy forms; after
this design the bodies of his chairs float free
from the frame. This became a distinguishing
feature of his work.

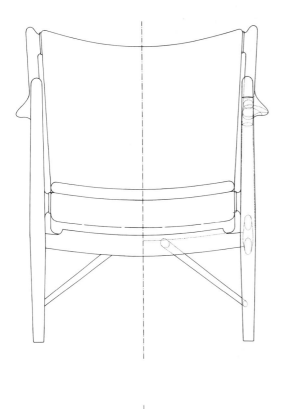

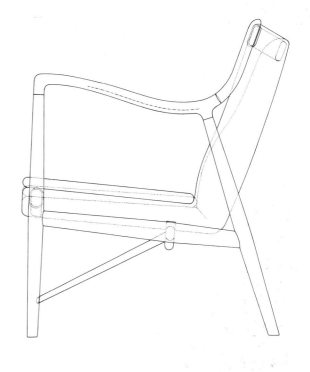

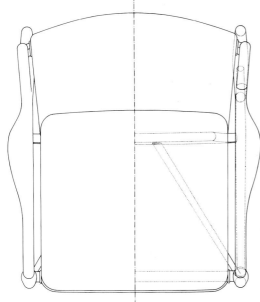

MATERIALS> Teak, Fabric
$16^{13}/_{32}$ x $30^{19}/_{32}$ x 32 / Sh $15^{19}/_{32}$ in. / 26.84 lbs.
660 x 765 x 800 / Sh 390 mm / 12.2 kg
MANUFACTURER> Bovirke

This chair shows the distinguishing features of Juhl's designs: the delicate curve of the arm and the seat floating free from the chair frame. The X-shaped crossbars under the finely detailed seat are the outstanding features of this chair. Another very similar chair was made by Niels Vodder.

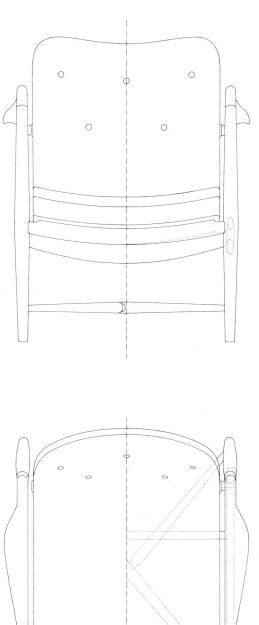

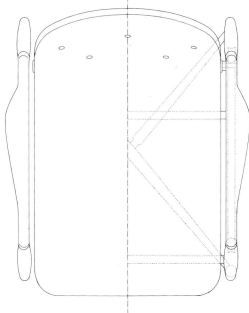

NAME>

EASY CHAIR

MATERIALS> Teak, Leather
28 x 25¹³/₃₂ x 31³/₁₆ / Sh 17¹⁹/₃₂ in. / 18.7 lbs.
700 x 635 x 780 / Sh 440 mm / 8.5 kg
MANUFACTURER> Niels Vodder, Søren Horn,
Niels Roth Andersen

Awarded a medal at the Milano Triennale, this chair is one of Juhl's most important designs. It was first produced by Niels Vodder. Production was suspended for several years until Niels Roth Andersen commenced production in 1991. This chair has a free-floating construction. In addition to this piece, a two-person chair was produced.

DESIGNER(S)>
FINN JUHL

NAME>
ARM CHAIR № 48

YEAR>
1948

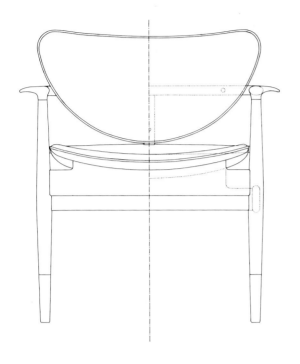

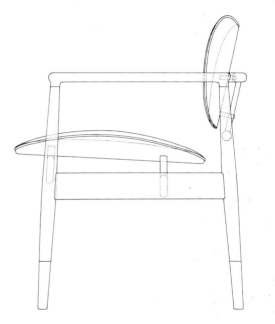

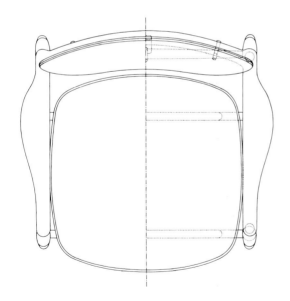

MATERIALS> Rosewood, Leather
41 x 36¹³/₃₂ x 37¹³/₃₂ / Sh 14³/₃₂ in. / 46.2 lbs.
1025 x 910 x 935 / Sh 352 mm / 21.0 kg
MANUFACTURER> Niels Vodder, Søren Horn, Niels
Roth Andersen

This is the most important of Finn Juhl's chair designs. It was shown at the Cabinetmakers' Guild Exhibition of 1949. Denmark's King Frederik is claimed to have sat on this chair at the exhibition, and so it was called the Chieftain Chair. Seventy-eight of these chairs were produced by Niels Vodder. Most were purchased by museums and by the Danish government for use in embassies in various parts of the world. The name Egyptian Chair comes from its construction, which is based on an old Egyptian chair.

Finn Juhl / Dining chair / 1949 / Niels Vodder, Niels Roth Andersen

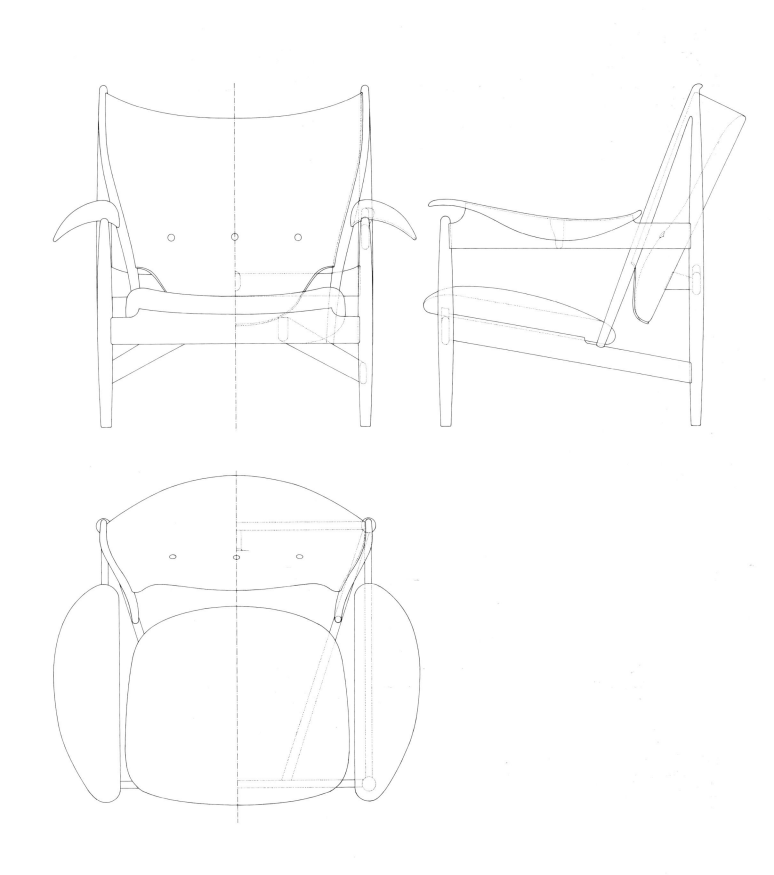

CHIEFTAIN CHAIR OR EGYPTIAN CHAIR

MATERIALS> Teak, Fabric
78 x 32$^{13}/_{16}$ x 38$^{13}/_{16}$ in.
1950 x 820 x 970 mm
MANUFACTURER> Niels Vodder, Baker Furniture

The wings fanning outward on either side make the sofa look bigger. It was shown at the 1950 Cabinetmakers' Guild Exhibition in conjunction with an arm chair and a nonsymmetrical table. Some models were mass-produced by Baker Furniture in the United States.

| DESIGNER(S)> | NAME> | YEAR> |
| FINN JUHL | SOFA | 1950 |

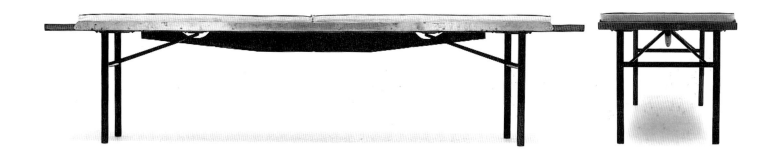

MATERIALS> Teak, Brass, Fabric
$73^{13}/_{32}$ x 18 x $17^{19}/_{32}$ / Sh $17^{19}/_{32}$ in. / 37.4 lbs.
1835 x 450 x 440 / Sh 440 mm / 17.0 kg
MANUFACTURER> Bovirke

This bench was actually used in Finn Juhl's home. The long, narrow cushion is designed so that it can be folded in half. The bench can also be used as a table. Two brass plates are inlaid to prevent the cushion from moving. The bottom portion of the legs are made of brass, enhancing the beauty of the piece.

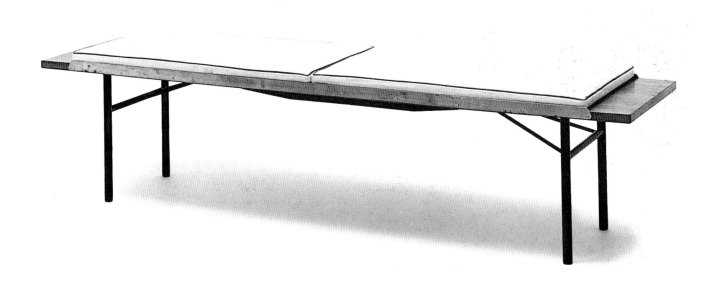

DESIGNER(S)>
FINN JUHL

NAME>
BENCH OR TABLE

YEAR>
1952

MATERIALS> Beech, Rosewood, Fabric
$29^3/_{16}$ x $28^{19}/_{32}$ x $35^{13}/_{32}$ / Sh 16 in. / 29.7 lbs.
730 x 715 x 885 / Sh 400 mm / 13.5 kg
MANUFACTURER> Bovirke

The sculptured feeling and elegance characterizing the works of Finn Juhl are prevalent in this chair. The portions of the piece that come in contact with hands and are easily soiled are made of dark rosewood, which will not show dirt. Danish furniture is designed not only with aesthetic aspects but also for functionality. This chair demonstrates these principles clearly.

DESIGNER(S)> FINN JUHL   NAME> EASY CHAIR   YEAR> 1952

MATERIALS> Beech, Teak, Fabric
32 x 31^{19}/$_{32}$ x 34 / Sh 14 in. / 35.64 lbs.
800 x 790 x 850 / Sh 350 mm / 16.2 kg
MANUFACTURER> Søren Willadsens Møbelfabrik

According to the research on Danish chairs, three of Finn Juhl's chair designs were released for public viewing by Søren Willadsens Co. This magnificent easy chair was one of those three designs. This chair is distinguished by its arms, which boldly wrap around the back. Though not particularly beautiful in appearance, this chair is noted for its comfort.

DESIGNER(S)>	NAME>	YEAR>
FINN JUHL	EASY CHAIR	1953

MATERIALS> Rosewood, Fabric
29 x 31³/₁₆ x 29¹⁹/₃₂ / Sh 14¹³/₁₆ in. / 28.82 lbs.
725 x 780 x 740 / Sh 370 mm / 13.1 kg
MANUFACTURER> Niels Vodder

The arms of this chair, which resemble an animal's horns, are its outstanding feature. The form is sculptured with delicate grooving and the seat rises slightly up from the frame. A sofa of this type was also designed.

Finn Juhl / Sofa / 1953 / Niels Vodder

DESIGNER(S)>
FINN JUHL

NAME>
EASY CHAIR N⁰ 53

YEAR>
1953

98

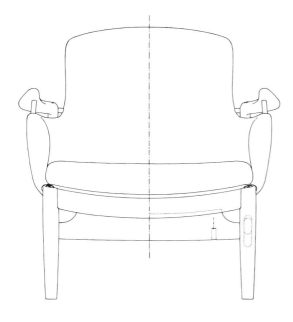

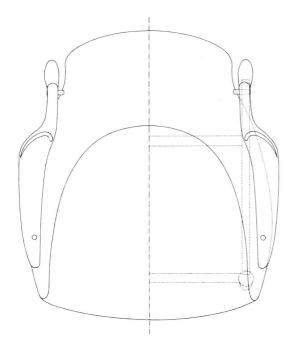

MATERIALS> Teak, Cane, Fabric, Brass
30 x 28¹³/₁₆ x 31¹³/₁₆ / Sh 15 in. / 21.2 lbs.
750 x 720 x 795 / Sh 375 mm / 9.6 kg
MANUFACTURER> Niels Vodder

Juhl designed several expandable tables and wall units but only one chair with a moveable back. The back can be moved to three positions and has curved laminated wood arms. When interviewed, Juhl claimed to have made only two chairs of this design, but at a later date the same chairs were put up for sale twice at auction, suggesting that these chairs were put into production without Juhl's permission.

Finn Juhl / Easy chair / ca. 1954 / Niels Vodder

DESIGNER(S)>
FINN JUHL

NAME>
EASY CHAIR

YEAR>
1953

100

MATERIALS> Teak, Leather
29^{19}/$_{32}$ x 31^{3}/$_{16}$ x 31^{3}/$_{16}$ / Sh 15^{23}/$_{32}$ in. / 18.92 lbs.
740 x 780 x 780 / Sh 393 mm / 8.6 kg
MANUFACTURER> France & Søn

This was the first chair Juhl designed for mass production. Although machine made, the organic curve that fits the human body makes this chair very comfortable.

DESIGNER(S)>
FINN JUHL   NAME>
ARM CHAIR   YEAR>
1954

101

HANS J.WEGNER

[DESIGNER] **1914–**

HANS J. WEGNER

Hans Jergensen Wegner was certified as a joiner in 1931. After starting his career as a furniture craftsman, he entered the joiner's course in the Technological Institute, where he graduated in 1938. He opened his own office in 1943. Demonstrating a deep understanding of furniture as a tool for everyday life, his designs are characterized by a dedication and adherence to functionality and comfort. His works are artistic and beautiful and at the same time practical and useful. He has thus succeeded in eliminating the apparent contradiction between these two worlds. Redesigning various pieces along the same themes was his unique talent; this enabled him to maintain a pace with the demands of an ever-changing world. His long career has established him as one of the most prolific designers in Denmark, and he has become famous internationally as well. His works grace the permanent collections of many of the world's most prestigious art museums.

HONORS> Lunning Prize, 1951. Grand Prix in the Milano Triennale, 1951. Diploe d'Honneur and gold medal, 1954. Silver medal, 1957. Eckersberg Medal, 1956. Copenhagen Cabinetmakers' Guild annual prize, 1959. Honorary Royal Designer of Industry, Royal Society of Arts, London, 1959. Citation of Merit, Pratt Institute, New York, 1959. American Institute of Decorators (for furniture design), 1961. International Design Award, 1961. Prince Eugene Medal, 1961. Copenhagen Cabinetmakers' Guild, annual prize and anniversary grant, 1965. International Design Award, American Institute of Interior Designers, 1968. Diploma di Collaborazione Triennale de Milano, 1973. Danish Furniture Prize, 1980. C. F. Hansen Medal, 1982. Danish Design Council annual prize, 1987.

MATERIALS> Beech
17 x 12 x 18¹⁹/₃₂ / Sh 10 in. / 7.7 lbs.
425 x 300 x 465 / Sh 250 mm / 3.5 kg
MANUFACTURER> Johannes Hansen Møbelsnedkeri,
Fredericia Stolefabrik

Wegner designed this chair as a gift for his god-
son, the son of his good friend Børge Mogensen.
The knockdown construction and the rounded
edges make it convenient as well as comfortable and safe for a child. The chair has been in
production for more than fifty years.

DESIGNER(S)>
HANS J. WEGNER

NAME>
PETER'S CHAIR

YEAR>
1943

MATERIALS> Cherry wood, Leather
22¹³/₁₆ x 22 x 32¹⁹/₃₂ / Sh 18³/₁₆ in. / 11 lbs.
570 x 550 x 815 / Sh 455 mm / 5.0 kg
MANUFACTURER> Fritz Hansens Eftf.

This famous chair is an adaptation of an old
Chinese chair from the Ming Dynasty. Its strong
construction makes it possible to have a seat
frame without a bar underneath. The curved top
rail consists of three parts joined by the finger-
joint technique. Its delicate curve and form
show superb craftsmanship. Wegner designed at
least nine Chinese chairs. This is an early work.

Hans J. Wegner / Chinese chair / 1945 / Fritz Hansens Eftf., PP
Møbler

DESIGNER(S)>	NAME>	YEAR>
HANS J. WEGNER	CHINESE CHAIR	1943

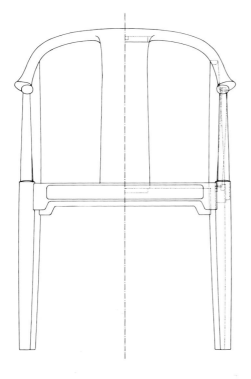

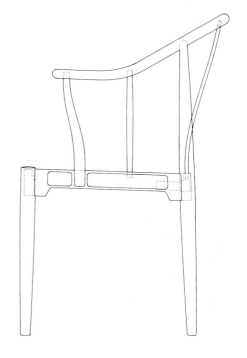

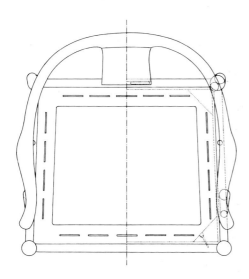

NAME>

CHINESE CHAIR

MATERIALS> Ash, Teak, Papercord
30¹³/₁₆ x 30¹³/₁₆ x 41³/₁₆ / Sh 14¹³/₃₂ in. / 17.16 lbs.
770 x 770 x 1030 / Sh 360 mm / 7.8 kg
MANUFACTURER> Johannes Hansen Møbelsnedkeri,
PP Møbler

Referred to as the Peacock Chair, the design of
this work was based on the old-English Windsor
chair. The name, based on the resemblance to
a peacock with its tail spread, was coined by
Finn Juhl, a close friend of the designer. The
expanding shape of the back as the lines move
upward gives the chair a magnanimous look. It
has also been called the Arrow Chair because
of the shape of the spokes of the back.

Hans J. Wegner / Easy chair (prototype) / 1953 / Johannes
Hansen Møbelsnedkeri

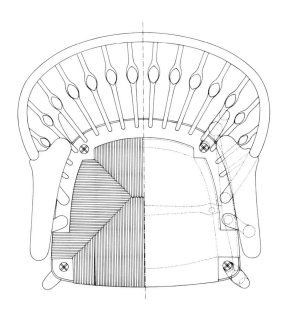

MATERIALS> Teak, Cane or Leather
$25^3/_{16}$ x $20^{13}/_{16}$ x $30^{13}/_{32}$ / Sh $17^{13}/_{16}$ in. / 10.56 lbs.
630 x 520 x 760 / Sh 445 mm / 4.8 kg
MANUFACTURER> Johannes Hansen Møbelsnedkeri,
PP Møbler

Of the many works designed by Wegner, this particular piece is arguably the most important. The chair is superior on several counts: the perfection of form, the comfort of the chair, the finishing of the details, and the use of materials. When this chair was unveiled in Denmark, it did not immediately gain renown. When it was featured in 1950 in the magazine *Interior,* the chair became famous. The chair is also famous as the one used by President John F. Kennedy. Kennedy, who suffered from back injuries, used this chair during his televised debates with Richard Nixon before the 1960 election. The chair was given its name (The Chair) by Osker Fitsher, director of the Den Parmanente (a well-known interior shop in Copenhagen) in 1950.

DESIGNER(S)>	NAME>	YEAR>
HANS J. WEGNER	THE CHAIR № 501	1949

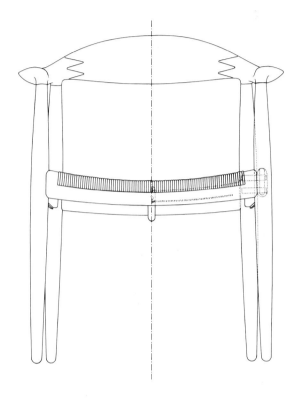
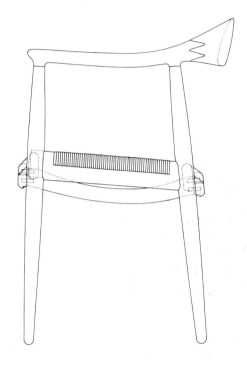
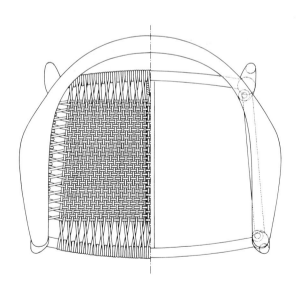

MATERIALS> Teak, Cane
24^{19}/$_{32}$ x 29^{3}/$_{16}$ x 30^{13}/$_{16}$ / Sh 15^{13}/$_{16}$ in. / 16.5 lbs.
615 x 730 x 770 / Sh 395 mm / 7.5 kg
MANUFACTURER> Johannes Hansen Møbelsnedkeri,
PP Møbler

This chair was shown at the Cabinetmakers'
Guild Exhibition of 1949, along with The Chair.
Its unique construction, with a seat frame
extending into the back legs and the back
frame into the front legs, makes the chair comfortable. It can be folded down and hung on
the wall, a construction design similar to one
found in old African chairs.

DESIGNER(S)>	NAME>		YEAR>
HANS J. WEGNER	FOLDING CHAIR	Nº 512	1949

MATERIALS> Oak, Cane
$28^{13}/_{16}$ x $30^{3}/_{16}$ x $30^{13}/_{16}$ / Sh $14^{13}/_{16}$ in. / 38.72 lbs.
720 x 755 x 770 / Sh 370 mm / 17.6 kg
MANUFACTURER> Carl Hansen & Søn

The seat frame of this easy chair extends to become the back legs in a design providing a great deal of comfort. In 1950, Wegner designed a different chair with the same construction but with a woven seat of papercord. The pattern made by the woven cane seat is a distinctive feature of this chair. The back has two "ears" formed by the shape of the corners. These "ears" were designed to act as hooks for a cushion or pillow to be attached.

Hans J. Wegner / Easy chair / Carl Hansen & Søn

| DESIGNER(S)> | NAME> | YEAR> |
| HANS J. WEGNER | EASY CHAIR № 27 | 1949 |

MATERIALS> Steel, Flag halyard
41$^{19}/_{32}$ x 46$^{31}/_{32}$ x 31$^{3}/_{16}$ / Sh 15$^{19}/_{32}$ in. / 38.52 lbs.
1040 x 1174 x 780 / Sh 390 mm / 26.6 kg
MANUFACTURER> Getama

This lounge chair is woven of flag halyard over a steel frame. In spite of its peculiar look (some say it resembles a space vehicle) it is very comfortable. Long-haired lamb skin is also used as the seat covering. The back pillow comes in two colors, orange or green.

DESIGNER(S)>	NAME>	YEAR>
HANS J. WEGNER	LOUNGE CHAIR №. 225	1950

MATERIALS> Oak, Papercord
22 x 20¹³/₁₆ x 29³/₁₆ / Sh 16¹³/₁₆ in. / 9.68 lbs.
550 x 520 x 730 / Sh 420 mm / 4.4 kg
MANUFACTURER> Carl Hansen & Søn

This is the best selling of Wegner's chairs. Wegner's Chinese chairs of 1943 and 1949 and his Y-chair of 1950 are related to this design. Perhaps one reason that this chair is so popular in Japan is that it has its roots in the Orient. The name Y-Chair is based on the Y-shaped construction of the back of the chair.

MATERIALS> Painted wood, Leather
23¹⁹/₃₂ x 18 x 29¹⁹/₃₂ / Sh 17⁷/₈ in. / 10.12 lbs.
590 x 450 x 740 / Sh 447 mm / 4.6 kg
MANUFACTURER> Johannes Hansen Møbelsnedkeri,
PP Møbler

Shown at the Cabinetmakers' Guild Exhibition
of 1952, this chair was given the name Cow
Horn Chair because of the beautiful, organic
curve of its arms. The joining wedges of the
top rail are another outstanding feature of this
piece. Most of the models which were produced for sale were made of finished wood.
The arms were designed to be shorter than is
usual so that the chair could function as a dining chair.

Hans J. Wegner / Arm chair / ca. 1987 / PP Møbler

DESIGNER(S)>
HANS J. WEGNER   NAME>
COW HORN CHAIR (PROTOTYPE)   YEAR>
1952

114

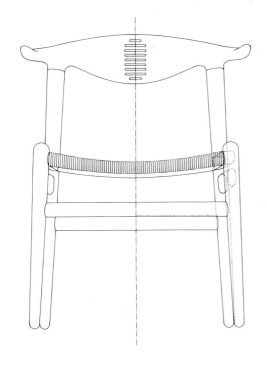

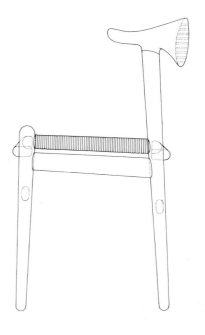

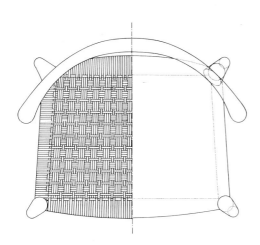

COW HORN CHAIR

MATERIALS> Oak
20 x 21³/₁₆ x 38 / Sh 17³/₁₆ in. / 13.64 lbs.
500 x 530 x 950 / Sh 430 mm / 6.2 kg
MANUFACTURER> Johannes Hansen Møbelsnedkeri,
PP Møbler

The back of this chair serves as a jacket hanger
and the seat, when upright, serves as a trousers
hanger. The box under the seat stores small
items of apparel. These functions provide its
name, Bachelor's Chair or Valet Chair. The
designer and Johannes Hansen and his craftsmen worked night and day for forty-eight hours
to have the chair ready for the show. It was
completed just three days before the exhibition. King Frederik greatly admired this chair
and ordered eight soon after the exhibition.

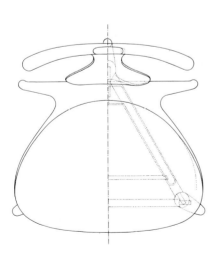

MATERIALS> Teak
$21^{19}/_{32}$ x $19^{13}/_{32}$ x $29^{3}/_{16}$ / Sh $16^{3}/_{16}$ in. / 7.7 lbs.
540 x 485 x 730 / Sh 405 mm / 3.5 kg
MANUFACTURER> Fritz Hansens Eftf.

Compared to the furniture designs of other countries, Danish designs include a high percentage of three-legged works. The floors of old houses in rural areas of Denmark are made of stone and earth and are unsteady for conventional four-legged furniture design. Three-legged, milk stool-type chairs are thus often found in these folk-style homes. The influence of this part of Danish culture and lifestyle is evident in the works of modern designers. This particular chair was designed as a set with a round table. The tapering seats facilitated their use around the table.

Hans J. Wegner / Arm chair / ca. 1981 / PP Møbler

DESIGNER(S)>	NAME>		YEAR>
HANS J. WEGNER	DINING CHAIR	№ 4103	1952

MATERIALS> Teak, Steel, Leather
$29^{19}/_{32}$ x 22 x $29^{3}/_{16}$ / Sh $17^{3}/_{16}$–20 in. / 30.8 lbs.
740 x 550 x 730 / Sh 430–500 mm / 14.0 kg
MANUFACTURER> Johannes Hansen Møbelsnedkeri

Wegner designed several chairs with casters, of which this is the most beautiful. Its distinctive features are its top rail design showing organic form and the strong finger joints between the top rail and arms. When first shown, the model had four steel-pipe legs. These were changed to four legs of die-cast steel and recently to five legs of die-cast steel.

MATERIALS> Teak, Cane
$28^{13}/_{16}$ x 20 x $28^{13}/_{16}$ / Sh $16^{13}/_{16}$ in. / 11 lbs.
720 x 500 x 720 / Sh 420 mm / 5.0 kg
MANUFACTURER> Johannes Hansen Møbelsnedkeri,
PP Møbler

To distinguish this chair from the Cow Horn
Chair, it was called the Bull Horn Chair. The
former chair has smaller arms with more curve
than the arms of this chair, which has large,
straight arms. The wedge used for the top rail
is the same on both chairs. The wedge con-
nects the materials on both sides and serves to
strengthen the structure of the chair as well as
enhance its beauty.

Hans J. Wegner / Dining chair / 1965 / Johannes Hansen
Møbelsnedkeri, PP Møbler

| DESIGNER(S)> | NAME> | | YEAR> | |
| HANS J. WEGNER | THE BULL HORN CHAIR | Nº 518 | 1960 | |

MATERIALS> Steel, Fabric
$39^{19}/_{32}$ x $39^{19}/_{32}$ x 36 / Sh $14^{3}/_{16}$ in. / 66 lbs.
30 x $21^{19}/_{32}$ x $14^{13}/_{32}$ / Sh $14^{13}/_{16}$ in. / 18.7 lbs.
990 x 990 x 900 / Sh 355 mm / 30.0 kg
750 x 54 x 360 / Sh 355 mm / 8.5 kg
MANUFACTURER> Johannes Hansen Møbelsnedkeri,
Erik Jørgensen Møbelfabrik A/S

One of Wegner's most important chairs, this
piece was created as an extension of the ideas
used in the Cow Horn Chair and the Bull Horn
Chair. Its special feature is the large headrest
that spreads out on each side. Combined with
the wide arms, it provides sitting comfort. Another
version of this chair, without the "wings," was
unveiled at the same time. Unfortunately, the
other version is no longer in production.

DESIGNER(S)>
HANS J. WEGNER

NAME>
THE OX CHAIR Nº 46   STOOL Nº 49

YEAR>
1960

121

MATERIALS> Painted wood
36³/₁₆ x 32¹³/₁₆ x 29³/₁₆ / Sh 18³/₁₆ in. / 25.3 lbs.
905 x 820 x 730 / Sh 455 mm / 11.5 kg
MANUFACTURER> Johannes Hansen Møbelsnedkeri

Shown in 1963 at the Cabinetmakers' Guild Exhibition, this chair was considered too radical. Twelve models were produced for the retrospective exhibition held to celebrate Wegner's seventy-seventh birthday in 1989. Photographs of the chair were picked for the cover of the catalogue of the exhibition.

DESIGNER(S)>
HANS J. WEGNER

NAME>
THREE-LEGGED SHELL CHAIR

YEAR>
1963

MATERIALS> Oak, Flag halyard, Fabric
29 x 73 x 27¹³/₁₆ / Sh 12¹⁹/₃₂ in. / 33.88 lbs.
725 x 1825 x 695 / Sh 315 mm / 15.4 kg
MANUFACTURER> Getama, PP Møbler

Hans J. Wegner created seven designs for the
chaise longue chairs. When this particular
chair was unveiled, it became the talk of the
industry. This chair was originally manufactured in oak by Getama Co., but a reproduction
of the work has recently been created in ash by
PP Møbler Co.

MATERIALS> Ash, Rosewood, Leather
23 x 19$^{13}/_{32}$ x 28$^{13}/_{16}$ / Sh 17 in. / 12.1 lbs.
575 x 485 x 720 / Sh 425 mm / 5.5 kg
MANUFACTURER> PP Møbler

Designed in 1965, the original sketch for this chair showed steel legs and a circular steel frame. Though the chair was never manufactured for sale, it was produced in 1986 with a laminated wood circular frame in accordance with the suggestion of the craftsmen making the chairs. Designers and craftsmen in Denmark hold positions of equal authority and responsibility; the opinions of each are carefully weighed and considered. This unique working arrangement has produced countless masterpieces. Indeed, this chair could never have been created without the suggestions and input from the craftsmen involved.

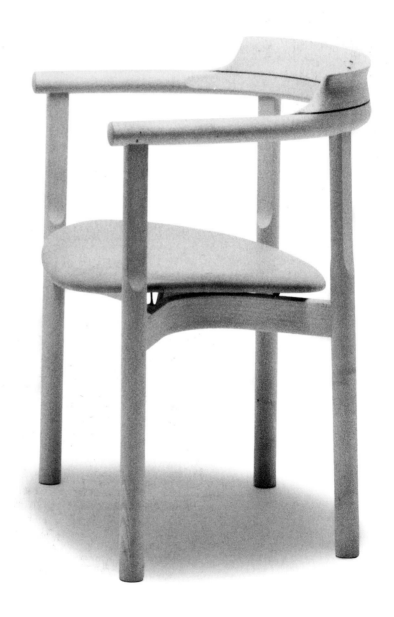

Hans J. Wegner / Arm chair / 1975 / PP Møbler

DESIGNER(S)>	NAME>	YEAR>
HANS J. WEGNER	ARM CHAIR № 55	1977

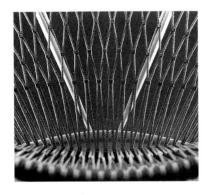

MATERIALS> Ash, Flag halyard, Fabric
45¹³/₃₂ x 37¹⁹/₃₂ x 38¹⁹/₃₂ / Sh 16¹⁹/₃₂ in. / 25.52 lbs.
1135 x 940 x 965 / Sh 415 mm / 11.6 kg
MANUFACTURER> PP Møbler

This chair was first designed in 1965. The
original sketch shows the leg portions and
the frame made of steel pipes. When it was
finally put into production in 1986, the production model was made of wood. At the
suggestion of the craftsmen, the wood was
laminated in a process in which thin pieces
of wood were layered and adhered under high
pressure. This chair is one example of how
the cooperation of craftsmen and designer is
essential to the creation of a masterpiece.

| DESIGNER(S)> | NAME> | YEAR> |
| HANS J. WEGNER | THE HOOP CHAIR | 1965 |

BØRGE**MOGENSEN**

[DESIGNER] **1914–1972**

BØRGE MOGENSEN

Børge Mogensen studied under Kaare Klint at the Royal Danish Academy of Fine Arts. Well versed in the theories and works of his mentor, he graduated from the Academy in the Department of Furniture Design in 1942. He served as the head of the furniture department of Denmark's Co-op from 1942 to 1950. His designs are characterized by an adherence to the concept of furniture for the common masses. The standardized dimensions of his designs paved the way for the development of component design of furniture, and he is credited with the first component-designed piece in the world. He served as a teaching assistant at the Royal Danish Academy of Fine Arts in the Department of Furniture Design from 1945 to 1947. After opening his own design office in 1950, he became one of the designers responsible for creating and maintaining the identity of Danish furniture.

HONORS> Eckersberg Medal, 1950. Copenhagen Cabinetmakers' Guild annual prize, 1958. Danish Furniture Prize, 1971. C. F. Hansen Medal, 1972. Royal Designer of Industry, London, 1972.

MATERIALS> Beech, Papercord
19¹³/₃₂ x 18¹³/₃₂ x 30 / Sh 17¹³/₁₆ in. / 9.9 lbs.
485 x 460 x 750 / Sh 445 mm / 4.5 kg
MANUFACTURER> F. D. B., Nordisk Anders-Eksport

Designed for the Farmer's Cooperative Association, this chair shows the influence of American Shaker furniture. The wide curve of the back and the simple construction of the chair itself make this piece particularly comfortable. It is one of the most important Danish furniture designs created for mass production. This masterpiece is often considered an equal to Hans J. Wegner's Y-Chair.

DESIGNER(S)>	NAME>	YEAR>
BØRGE MOGENSEN	SHAKER CHAIR, J-39	1944

MATERIALS> Oak, Leather
30 x 34 x 26¹³/₁₆ / Sh 11 in. / 19.8 lbs.
750 x 850 x 670 / Sh 275 mm / 9.0 kg
MANUFACTURER> Erhard Rasmussen, Fredericia
Stolefabrik

In 1950, this chair, along with a dining chair
and table, was shown at the Cabinetmakers'
Guild Exhibition. The theme of this exhibition was "Hunting Lodge." The frame of the
seat serves as the back legs and the seat
itself is low and comfortable. In 1954, Carlo
Mollino designed a chair of similar construction, probably an adaptation of this chair.

Børge Mogensen / Easy chair / 1955 / Fredericia Stolefabrik

DESIGNER(S)>	NAME>	YEAR>
BØRGE MOGENSEN	HUNTING CHAIR	1950

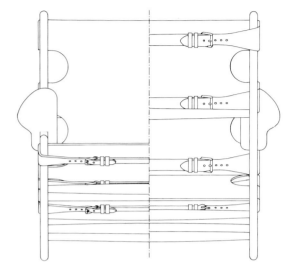

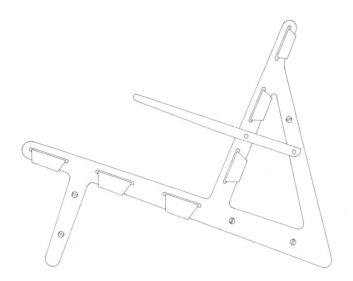

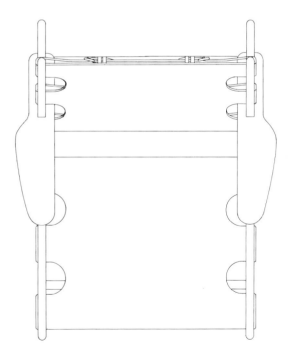

MATERIALS> Oak, Leather

$22^{19}/_{32}$ x $20^{13}/_{32}$ x $32^{3}/_{16}$ / Sh 17 in. / 14.3 lbs.

565 x 510 x 805 / Sh 425 mm / 6.5 kg

MANUFACTURER> Erhard Rasmussen, Fredericia Stolefabrik

An extension of his Hunting Chair design, this chair demonstrates Mogensen's bold use of materials and delicate design detail. The front frame of the seat is curved inward for comfortable sitting. The leather seat back can be tightened with a belt if the leather stretches. The leather seat can also be adjusted. This highly perfected piece demonstrates good design in both proportion and function.

DESIGNER(S)>	NAME>	YEAR>
BØRGE MOGENSEN	DINING CHAIR	1951

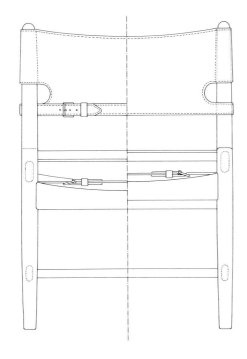

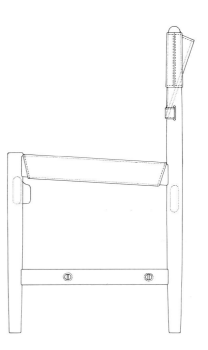

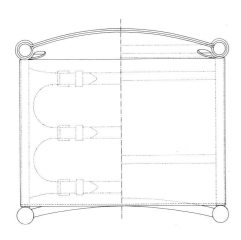

DINING CHAIR

MATERIALS> Oak, Cane, Fabric
26¹³/₃₂ x 33¹⁹/₃₂ x 37 / Sh 14¹³/₃₂ in. / 20.9 lbs.
660 x 840 x 925 / Sh 360 mm / 9.5 kg
MANUFACTURER> Erhard Rasmussen, Fredericia
Stolefabrik

The origin of this chair's design is the wing-back chair. The seat slides forward to adjust the angle of the seat to the back for greater comfort. The early model had a woven cane back and later ones have a back of laminated veneer.

Børge Mogensen / Easy chair, stool / ca. 1960 / Fredericia Stolefabrik

DESIGNER(S)>	NAME>	YEAR>
BØRGE MOGENSEN	HIGHBACK EASY CHAIR	1956

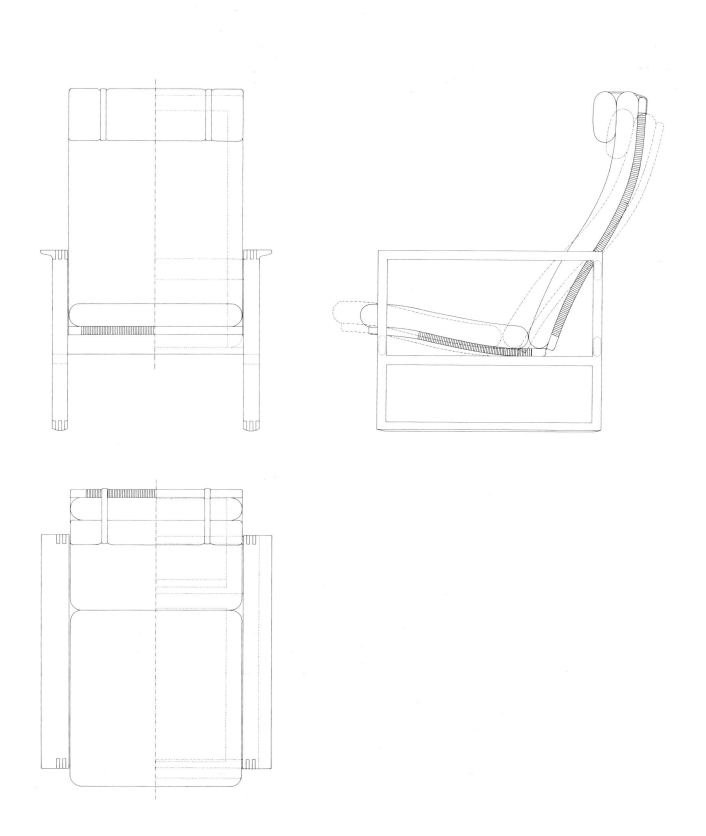

MATERIALS> Oak, Leather
68 x 19^{19}/$_{32}$ x 30^{13}/$_{32}$ / Sh 17^{3}/$_{16}$ in. / 39.82 lbs.
1700 x 490 x 760 / Sh 430 mm / 18.1 kg
MANUFACTURER> Fredericia Stolefabrik

This adaptation of a Shaker chair was designed as a bench as well as a dining chair. By extending the side of the dining chair, a bench is created. The bench vividly expresses the design concept, with the back a beautifully proportioned single piece of wood. The seat is a single piece of leather with no seams.

DESIGNER(S)>   NAME>   YEAR>
BØRGE MOGENSEN   **BENCH**   1956

MATERIALS> Oak, Cane
24 x 19 x 30 / Sh 17^{19}/$_{32}$ in. / 11.44 lbs.
600 x 475 x 750 / Sh 440 mm / 5.2 kg
MANUFACTURER> P. Lauritsen, Fredericia Stolefabrik

This chair was produced by Fredericia Stolefabrik after P. Lauritsen & Søn went out of
business. A few of the models produced had
cane seats and backs. A cross bar connecting
the front and back legs at floor level character-
izes the chair. This construction is especially
good for soft floors.

Børge Mogensen / Dining chair / 1959 / P. Lauritsen,
Fredericia Stolefabrik

DESIGNER(S)>
BØRGE MOGENSEN

NAME>
ARM CHAIR

YEAR>
1957

MATERIALS> Oak, Leather
33³/₁₆ x 24¹³/₁₆ x 27³/₁₆ / Sh 14¹³/₁₆ in. / 26.4 lbs.
830 x 620 x 680 / Sh 370 mm / 12.0 kg
MANUFACTURER> Fredericia Stolefabrik

The back and seat of this chair are fastened by thick leather straps, a design popular in old Spanish chairs. The overall impression of this chair is forceful, yet it also has excellent details. Mogensen's works are characterized by a strong, simple presence, beautiful lines, and a high level of comfort.

DESIGNER(S)>
BØRGE MOGENSEN

NAME>
SPANISH CHAIR

YEAR>
1959

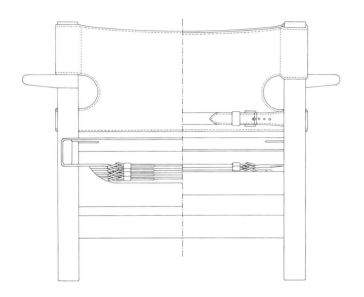

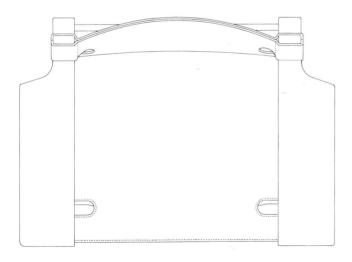

MATERIALS> Teak, Leather
$24^{13}/_{32}$ x $20^9/_{16}$ x $28^{13}/_{32}$ / Sh $17^{27}/_{32}$ in. / 15.18 lbs.
610 x 505 x 710 / Sh 446 mm / 6.9 kg
MANUFACTURER> Fredericia Stolefabrik

The distinctive feature of this chair is the wide back supported by the back legs. The upholstered and padded back is designed to provide extra comfort. Similar chairs have been designed by Hans J. Wegner.

DESIGNER(S)>
BØRGE MOGENSEN

NAME>
CONFERENCE CHAIR

YEAR>
1962

138

MATERIALS> Teak, Leather
28 x 35^{19}/$_{32}$ x 42^{13}/$_{32}$ / Sh 17^{13}/$_{32}$ in. / 63.8 lbs.
700 x 890 x 1060 / Sh 435 mm / 29.0 kg
MANUFACTURER> Fredericia Stolefabrik

Mogensen began designing wingback chairs in 1939 and many of his designs are adaptations of eighteenth-century English chairs. This version demonstrates the influence of Klint and also shows innovation. Klint's wingback chairs were almost identical to the English chairs, whereas this design exhibits Mogensen's originality.

DESIGNER(S)>	NAME>	YEAR>
BØRGE MOGENSEN	WINGBACK CHAIR	1964

AKSELBENDERMADSEN

[DESIGNER] **1916–**

EJNERLARSEN

[DESIGNER] **1917–1987**

AKSEL BENDER MADSEN

Journeyman joiner (silver medal), 1936. Graduated from the School of Arts, Crafts, and Design, Department of Furniture Design, 1940. Studied at the Royal Danish Academy of Fine Arts, Department of Furniture Design. Employed by Kaare Klint and Arne Jacobsen, 1940–43. Associate with Co-op Denmark's architect office, 1943–50. Associated with the Copenhagen Municipal Architect since 1954. Teacher at the School of Arts, Crafts, and Design, Department of Furniture Design, 1946–54. Inspector of the School of Arts, Crafts, and Design, 1950–54. Own office with Ejner Larsen since 1947.

HONORS> Prizes in a number of competitions and others for arts and crafts. Cabinetmakers' Guild annual prize, 1956 and 1961.

EJNER LARSEN

Trained as a craftsman. Graduated from the School of Arts, Crafts, and Design, Department of Furniture Design, 1940. Teacher at the school, 1942–57. Worked under Jacob Kjær, architect Mogens Koch, Palle Suenson, 1942–52. Architect at Christiansborg Palace, 1952–70. Court and state inventory inspector, 1977. Own office with A. Bender Madsen since 1947.

HONORS> Bronze and silver medals for competition for craftsmen. Cabinetmakers' Guild annual prize, 1956, 1961.

MATERIALS> Teak, Leather
$30^{19}/_{32}$ x 22 x $31^{13}/_{32}$ / Sh 17 in. / 22 lbs.
765 x 550 x 785 / Sh 425 mm / 10.0 kg
MANUFACTURER> Willy Beck, Søro Stolefabric

This important product of the two designers features a wide back that becomes the arms. The seat is light and the frame is thinner in the center than the sides. The chair's simple construction invokes a modern feeling.

MATERIALS> Teak, Leather
$20^{13}/_{16}$ x $20^{13}/_{32}$ x $31^{3}/_{16}$ / Sh $17^{11}/_{16}$ in. / 13.86 lbs.
520 x 510 x 780 / Sh 442 mm / 6.3 kg
MANUFACTURER> Willy Beck

Although these designers worked together primarily for the Willy Beck Company, they also produced furniture for Fritz Hansens Eftf. during a brief period. This arm chair maintains the characteristics of similar chairs produced before it, distinguished by the slender pieces of the seat frame. This particular chair is also characterized by the detail of joining the back legs and top rail.

Aksel B. Madsen / Ejner Larsen / Dining chair / ca. 1950 / Fritz Hansens Eftf.

DESIGNER(S)>	NAME>	YEAR>
AKSEL BENDER MADSEN / EJNER LARSEN	ARM CHAIR	CA. 1950

MATERIALS> Teak, Cane
50¹³/₃₂ x 20 x 38 / Sh 14¹³/₃₂ in. / 37.4 lbs.
1260 x 500 x 950 / Sh 360 mm / 17.0 kg
MANUFACTURER> Willy Beck, Søro Stolefabric

This easy chair for two is the most important collaboration of the two designers. They also designed a single-seat chair, but this two-seat version has better proportions. The detached curve of the front seat frame is characteristic of their work.

| DESIGNER(S)> | NAME> | YEAR> |
| AKSEL BENDER MADSEN / EJNER LARSEN | EASY CHAIR | 1960 |

KAI**CHRISTIANSEN**

[DESIGNER] **1916–**

KAI CHRISTIANSEN

Journeyman joiner, 1949. Completed his studies with Kaare Klint at the Royal Danish Academy of Fine Arts, 1950. Opened his own office in 1955.

MATERIALS> Teak, Cane, Fabric
29 x 32^{13}/$_{32}$ x 34^{13}/$_{16}$ / Sh 13^{13}/$_{16}$ in. / 36.3 lbs.
725 x 810 x 870 / Sh 345 mm / 16.5 kg
MANUFACTURER> Chr. Jensen

This chair was designed using straight lines, emphasizing its simple, straight form. The use of cane for the back gives the appearance of softness. This chair is a good example of Danish furniture design.

HELGEVESTERGAARDJENSEN

[DESIGNER] **1917–87**

HELGE VESTERGAARD JENSEN

Apprentice joiner, 1937. Graduated from the School of Arts, Crafts, and Design, Department of Furniture Design, 1943. Worked with Hvidt & Mølgaard Nielsen, 1944–46; Palle Suenson, 1946–48; and Vilhelm Lauritzen, 1948–50. Opened his own office in 1950.

HONORS> Prizes for furniture design, 1954, 1955, 1957, 1958, 1960, 1961, 1962, and 1963.

MATERIALS> Teak, Leather
24¹³/₁₆ x 21¹³/₁₆ x 35¹³/₁₆ / Sh 17¹⁹/₃₂ in. / 17.38 lbs.
620 x 545 x 895 / Sh 440 mm / 7.9 kg
MANUFACTURER> Peder Pedersen

This chair was entered in the 1958
Cabinetmakers' Guild Exposition together with
a set of armless dining chairs, an oval table,
and a sideboard. The chair immediately
became the talk of the industry. It is characterized by organic curves comprising the lines
of the piece. The curves are designed to fit
against the backbone of the person sitting in
the chair, providing comfort and support.

DESIGNER(S)>
HELGE VESTERGAARD JENSEN

NAME>
ARM CHAIR

YEAR>
1958

MATERIALS> Walnut, Nyloncord, Leather
29^{19}/$_{32}$ x 33^{3}/$_{16}$ x 45^{13}/$_{64}$ / Sh 16^{13}/$_{16}$ in. / 17.82 lbs.
740 x 830 x 1130 / Sh 420 mm / 8.1 kg
MANUFACTURER> Peder Pedersen, Søren Horn,
Niels Roth Andersen

Called the Racket Chair because nylon cord was
used for the seat and back. Jensen designed a
series of furniture, including a bed and a highback chair, using the same materials. The first
model of this chair was woven from bottom to top
and had a cylindrical headrest.

DESIGNER(S)>
HELGE VESTERGAARD JENSEN   NAME>   RACKET CHAIR   YEAR>   1955

MATERIALS> Mahogany, Leather
23³/₁₆ x 21³/₁₆ x 37¹³/₁₆ / Sh 17.68 in. / 13.2 lbs.
580 x 530 x 945 / Sh 442 mm / 6.0 kg
MANUFACTURER> Søren Horn, Niels Roth Andersen

Designed for formal dining, this chair's outstanding feature is its elegant, beautifully
curved back line. The absence of a supporting
crossbar under the seat requires excellent
craftsmanship.

Helge V. Jensen / Dining chair / 1963 / Søren Horn, Niels Roth
Andersen

DESIGNER(S)>
HELGE VESTERGAARD JENSEN

NAME>
DINING CHAIR

YEAR>
1963

EBBE**CLEMMENSEN**
[ARCHITECT, PROFESSOR] **1917–**

KAREN**CLEMMENSEN**
[ARCHITECT, DESIGNER] **1917–**

EBBE CLEMMENSEN

Graduated from the Royal Danish Academy of Fine Arts, Institute of Building Design, 1941. Worked for E.G. Poul Holsoe and Fritz Schlegel. Opened his own office in 1946 with Karen Clemmensen. Teacher of building design, the Royal Danish Academy of Fine Arts, 1962; professor since 1964.

HONORS> Prizes for building in Gentofte, Gladsaxe, and Helsingor Municipalities. The Neuhausen Prize, 1949. The Academy's Gold Medal, 1950. Eckersberg Medal, 1961. Wood Prize, 1968. Diploma from the Association for the Beautification of the Capital, 1969.

KAREN CLEMMENSEN

Graduated from the Royal Danish Academy of Fine Arts, Institute of Building Design, 1942. Employed by Professor K. Gottlob, 1939–41; by design office in Stockholm, 1943–45; by the Copenhagen Municipal Architect, 1946. Opened own office in 1946 with Ebbe Clemmensen.

HONORS> Prizes for building in Gentofte, Gladsaxe, and Helsingor Municipalities. Various Danish grants. Eckersberg Medal, 1961. Wood Prize, 1968. Diploma from the Association for the Beautification of the Capital, 1969.

MATERIALS> Ash, Fabric, Leather
24¹³/₃₂ x 27¹⁹/₃₂ x 28¹³/₁₆ / Sh 14³/₁₆ in. / 19.8 lbs.
610 x 690 x 720 / Sh 355 mm / 9.0 kg
MANUFACTURER> Fritz Hansens Eftf.

A representative chair of Danish design. The leg section is triangular, providing strong, lightweight construction. The finishing details of the arms and legs are reminiscent of the Safari Chair designed by Klint. The detail is particularly fine.

DESIGNER(S)>
EBBE CLEMMENSEN / KAREN CLEMMENSEN

NAME>
EASY CHAIR № 4305

YEAR>
1963

149

JØRN**UTZON**

[ARCHITECT] **1918–**

JØRN UTZON

Graduated from the Royal Danish Academy of Fine Arts, Department of Architecture, 1942. Maintains his own office.

HONORS> Various Danish grants. The Academy's small gold medal, 1947. Bissen Prize, 1947. Eckersberg Medal, 1957. Bund Deutscher Archiektens Ehrenplacette, 1965. C. F. Hansen Medal, 1967. Danish Furniture Prize, 1970. Honorary member of the American Institute of Architects, 1978. The Royal Institute of British Architects' Gold Medal, 1978. The Order of Australia, 1985.

MATERIALS> Maple, Steel, Fabric
30 x 38^{13}/$_{16}$ x 36^{13}/$_{16}$ / Sh 14^{3}/$_{32}$ in. / 62.92 lbs.
750 x 970 x 920 / Sh 352 mm / 28.6 kg
MANUFACTURER> Fritz Hansens Eftf.

Utzon, a world-famous architect, designed the Opera House in Sydney, Australia. The side view of this chair shows its dynamic curvature. The production model of this prototype has a different leg design.

DESIGNER(S)>	NAME>	YEAR>
JØRN UTZON	LOUNGE CHAIR (PROTOTYPE)	1968

MATERIALS> Aluminum, Fabric
31 x 29^{13}/$_{32}$ x 28^{13}/$_{32}$ / Sh 17^{13}/$_{32}$ in. / 53.9 lbs.
775 x 735 x 710 / Sh 435 mm / 24.5 kg
MANUFACTURER> Fritz Hansens Eftf.

An extremely striking piece, this chair is distinguished by the frame construction. A well-known, female architect and designer named Gae Aulenti created a chair with the same construction, which she unveiled under the auspices of the Knoll International Co. in the United States in 1975. Gae Aulenti's chair was produced with cushions on the back and seat but not the arms. She also designed an easy chair and a dining chair in the same series. Utzon's variations of this chair include a sofa bed-type chair characterized by the extension of the seat.

| DESIGNER(S)> | NAME> | YEAR> |
| JØRN UTZON | **EASY CHAIR** | 1968 |

GUNNARAAGAARDANDERSEN

[PROFESSOR, ARTIST] **1919–82**

GUNNAR AAGAARD ANDERSEN

Studied at the School of Arts, Crafts, and Design, 1936–39. Studied at the Royal Danish Academy of Fine Arts, 1939–46. Professor at the Royal Danish Academy of Fine Arts from 1972. Vice president of the Academy, 1973–74.

HONORS> Denmark's National Bank's Anniversary Foundation of 1968; other Danish grants.

MATERIALS> Ash, Leather
$18^{59}/_{64}$ x $8^{13}/_{16}$ x $11^{13}/_{16}$ in.
473 x 220 x 295 mm
MANUFACTURER> Ivan Schlecter

This uniquely designed piece provides an arm or back rest for a standing person. It demonstrates a concept similar to the traditional Japanese elbow rest, called the *kyosoku*, designed for use on Japanese tatami mats. The *kyosoku* was used in Japan by samurai of high position. This work is an interesting example of a traditional Japanese article appearing in Denmark in altered form.

DESIGNER(S)>	NAME>	YEAR>
GUNNAR AAGAARD ANDERSEN	STANDING CHAIR	DESIGN YEAR UNKNOWN

MATERIALS> Ash
24 x 19³/₁₆ x 29¹⁹/₃₂ / Sh 16²³/₃₂ in. / 15.40 lbs.
600 x 480 x 740 / Sh 418 mm / 7.0 kg
MANUFACTURER> Søren Horn, Niels Roth Andersen

Demonstrating a simple yet innovating idea, this chair's seat and back are composed of pieces of wood. These thin pieces of wood are not fixed, providing elasticity and comfortable seating. The chair received a prize from the Danish Furniture Design Committee. Only a few prototypes were made and it has yet to be mass produced.

DESIGNER(S)>
GUNNAR AAGAARD ANDERSEN

NAME>
SIDE CHAIR (PROTOTYPE)

YEAR>
1979

ILLUM**WIKKELSØ**

[DESIGNER] **1919–**

ILLUM WIKKELSØ

Journeyman joiner, 1938. Graduated from the School of Arts, Crafts, and Design, 1941. Employed by cabinetmaker Jacob Kjær and architect Hvidt & Mølgaard. Opened his own office in 1954.

MATERIALS> Rosewood, Cane, Fabric
$29^{19}/_{32}$ x $27^{3}/_{16}$ x $29^{13}/_{16}$ / Sh $17^{19}/_{32}$ in. / 25.3 lbs.
740 x 680 x 745 / Sh 440 mm / 11.5 kg
MANUFACTURER> C. F. Christensen

The distinctive features of this chair are the arms that curve outward and the back that curves backward. It is made from three frames of the same shape and connected by screws. Swedish designer Arne Knoell has made a chair of a similar design.

DESIGNER(S)>
ILLUM WIKKELSØ

NAME>
EASY CHAIR

YEAR>
DESIGN YEAR UNKNOWN

154

HANS**OLSEN**

[DESIGNER] **1919–**

HANS OLSEN

Journeyman joiner, 1941. Graduated from the School of Arts, Crafts, and Design, 1943. Opened his own office in 1953.
HONORS> Gold medal at California State Fair, 1961. International Design Award, 1965.

MATERIALS> Teak, Leather
$19^{13}/_{16}$ x $18^{13}/_{32}$ x 28 / Sh $17^{11}/_{16}$ in. / 8.14 lbs.
495 x 460 x 700 / Sh 442 mm / 3.7 kg
MANUFACTURER> Frem Røjle

This chair is designed to use with a round table. Five of these chairs make a circle when arranged together. A four-legged model was also designed.

DESIGNER(S)>	NAME>	YEAR>
HANS OLSEN	DINING CHAIR	1952

GRETE**JALK**

[DESIGNER] **1922–**

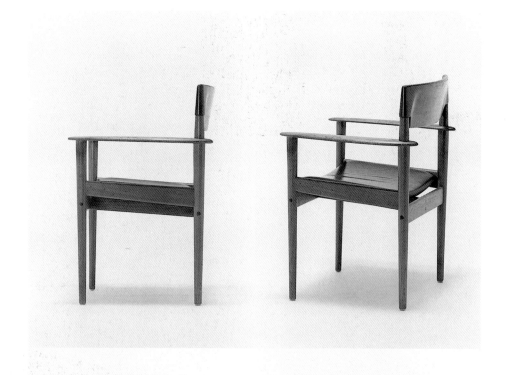

GRETE JALK

Apprentice joiner, 1940–43. Graduated from the School of Arts, Crafts, and Design, 1946. Teacher at the School of Arts, Crafts, and Design, Department of Furniture Design, 1955–60. Opened her own office in 1954. Co-editor of the periodical *MOBILIA,* 1956–62 and 1968–74. Member of the Danish Design Council, 1981, and of the Council's ID Prize jury, 1977 and 1979–87. Organized a number of traveling exhibitions for the Ministry of Foreign Affairs. Editor of *Dunsk Mobelkunst Gennem 40 Aar* (Forty Years of Danish Furniture Design), published 1987.

HONORS> First prize, Cabinetmakers' competition, 1946 and 1963. First prize, Georg Jensen competition, 1953. First prize, Brdr. Dahl Wallpaper competition, 1955. Daily Mail International Furniture Competition, 1963. Cabinetmakers' Guild Prize, 1961, 1963. Danish State Art Foundation, 1981.

MATERIALS> Rosewood, Leather
29³/₁₆ x 34¹⁹/₃₂ x 37³/₁₆ / Sh 13¹³/₁₆ in. / 36.3 lbs.
730 x 865 x 930 / Sh 345 mm / 16.5 kg
MANUFACTURER> P. Jeppesens Møbelfabrik
A/S

One of the few women furniture designers, Grete Jalk worked at a number of well-known furniture-producing companies, including Henning Jensen's studio, Fritz Hansens Eftf., France & Søn, and Søren Horn. She was most prolific at P. Jeppesen's studio, producing many fine pieces. Her works are characterized by certain hidden details that can be seen in the joints of the back leg and arm portions of this chair. The legs pass through holes in the arms of the chair. To prevent the arms from dropping too low, the legs below the hole are wider. The innovative top rail design covers the tops of the legs for added support.

Grete Jalk / Easy chair / ca. 1960 / France & Søn

DESIGNER(S)>
GRETE JALK

NAME>
EASY CHAIR

YEAR>
1956

MATERIALS> Mahogany, Leather
16 x 16 x 26¹³/₁₆ / Sh 26⁷/₈–34¹⁹/₃₂ in. / 14.3 lbs.
500 x 400 x 670 / Sh 854–672 mm / 6.5 kg
MANUFACTURER> Henning Jensen, Søren Horn,
Niels Roth Andersen

Designed to be used with a writing table, the
height of the stool's seat is adjusted easily by
the screw mechanism. The cut-ends of the
legs, with a gentle curve and a sharp edge, are
a distinctive feature of this stool. It is not an
exaggeration to say that this stool will be
remembered as a masterpiece in Danish furniture making history.

DESIGNER(S)>	NAME>	YEAR>
GRETE JALK	STOOL	1961

MATERIALS> Teak
$25^{3}/_{16}$ x $28^{13}/_{16}$ x 30 / Sh $13^{3}/_{32}$ in. / 12.1 lbs.
630 x 720 x 750 / Sh 327 mm / 5.5 kg
MANUFACTURER> P. Jeppesens Møbelfabrik A/S

This chair received first prize in the furniture
competition sponsored by the *Daily Mirror*
newspaper. A prototype made earlier was unfortunately lost when the P. Jeppesens company
burned. This work established Jalk as a designer
of renown. This excellent laminated design was
intended for mass production but the chair was
considered too radical and was therefore not
put into production.

| DESIGNER(S)> | NAME> | YEAR> |
| GRETE JALK | LAMINATED CHAIR | 1963 |

NIELS**O.MØLLER**

[DESIGNER] **1920–**

NIELS O. MØLLER

Journeyman joiner, 1939. Independent designer and manufacturer since 1944. Director of J. L. Møllers Møbel-fabrik A/S.

HONORS> Danish Furniture Manufacturers Association's Foundation Fair Award, 1975.

MATERIALS> Rosewood
$22^{13}/_{32}$ x $20^{13}/_{32}$ x $32^{3}/_{16}$ / Sh $17^{19}/_{32}$ in. / 10.12 lbs.
560 x 510 x 805 / Sh 440 mm / 4.6 kg
MANUFACTURER> J. L. Møller

Although mostly made by machine, this chair has a hand-crafted quality because the details have been finished by craftsmen. The design itself is ageless, and a masterpiece such as this can and should be used throughout one's entire life. In Denmark, works such as these are treasured and used carefully and many pieces are passed from generation to generation. If a chair is damaged, it can be restored to its original condition. The timelessness of this chair lies not only in its construction but also in its design.

Niels O. Møller / Dining chair / 1976 / J. L. Møller

DESIGNER(S)>	NAME>	YEAR>
NIELS O. MØLLER	DINING CHAIR	1976

VILHELM**WOHLERT**

[ARCHITECT] 1920–

VILHELM WOHLERT

Vilhelm Wohlert studied under Kay Fisker at the Royal Danish Academy of Fine Arts, graduating in 1944. He served as an instructor of architecture at the Academy from 1944–46 and again from 1953–56. He opened his own architecture office in 1948 and served as a professor at the School of Architecture from 1968. He was vice president of the Royal Danish Academy of Fine Arts from 1968 to 1970. Vilhelm Wohlert designed furniture for Arne Poulsen and Ludvig Pontoppidan and for Soløfabrik as well as for museums and institutions.

HONORS> Royal Danish Academy of Fine Arts Gold Medal, 1946. Eckersberg Medal, 1958. C. F. Hansen Medal, 1979.

MATERIALS> Painted wood
$18^{13}/_{16}$ x $18^{13}/_{32}$ x $29^{19}/_{32}$ / Sh $17^{13}/_{32}$ in. / 6.82 lbs.
470 x 460 x 740 / Sh 435 mm / 3.1 kg
MANUFACTURER> P. Jeppesens Møbelfabrik A/S

The emphasis on construction characterizing this piano chair strongly suggests the work of a master architect. The height of the seat is thought to be adjustable by the metal fittings hidden under the seat. The year of the design is unknown, though it frequently appeared in exhibitions introducing Danish furniture during 1956. The designer, in conjunction with Jørgen Bohr, designed the world-famous Louisiana Museum of Art, an excellent example of Danish design.

DESIGNER(S)>	NAME>	YEAR>
VILHELM WOHLERT	PIANO CHAIR	CA. 1955

IB**KOFOD-LARSEN**

[DESIGNER] **1921–**

IB KOFOD-LARSEN

Graduated Royal Danish Academy of Fine Arts.
HONORS> Cabinetmakers' Guild annual prize.
Holmegaard glass competition, 1948.

MATERIALS> Teak, Fabric
25 x 26¹³/₁₆ x 30³/₁₆ / Sh 15¹⁹/₃₂ in. / 18.04 lbs.
625 x 670 x 755 / Sh 390 mm / 8.2 kg
MANUFACTURER> Christensen & Larsen Møbelhåndværk

The distinctive features of this chair are its large back and the joinery of the back and legs. Shown at the Cabinetmakers' Guild Exhibition in 1950, this construction employs a treatment similar to that used by Finn Juhl in his Chieftain Chair. The designer has unveiled several variations of this easy chair, some with tacks and others with steel pipes.

Ib Kofod-Larsen / Easy chair / ca. 1950 / Christensen & Larsen
Møbelhåndværk

DESIGNER(S)>	NAME>	YEAR>
IB KOFOD-LARSEN	EASY CHAIR	1950

MATERIALS> Mahogany, Leather
30^{13}/$_{16}$ x 29^{3}/$_{16}$ x 29^{3}/$_{16}$ / Sh 15 in. / 30.8 lbs.
13^{19}/$_{32}$ x 22^{13}/$_{16}$ x 14 / Sh 13^{19}/$_{32}$ in. / 11.88 lbs.
770 x 730 x 730 / Sh 375 mm / 14.0 kg
340 x 570 x 350 / Sh 340 mm / 5.4 kg
MANUFACTURER> Christensen & Larsen Møbelhåndværk

One of Kofod-Larsen's most important models, this chair was shown at the Cabinetmakers' Guild Exhibition of 1956 along with a bed and sofa. The sculpture-like form has great beauty and elegance. Piet Hain's poem "The Chair and a Sculpture" was written about this chair.

NANNA**DITZEL**
[DESIGNER] **1923–**

JØRGEN**DITZEL**
[DESIGNER] **1921–61**

NANNA DITZEL

Graduated from the School of Arts, Crafts, and Design, 1946. Opened an office with Jørgen Ditzel in 1946, where they worked together until Jørgen Ditzel's death in 1961. Member of the board of the Furniture Maker's Autumn Exhibition (SE), the Georg Jensen Foundation, and the Danish Design Council.

HONORS> Good Design Award, 1953. Silver medal, Milano Triennale, 1951, 1954, and 1957. Lunning Prize (with Jørgen Ditzel), 1956. Gold medal, Milano Triennale, 1960.

JØRGEN DITZEL

Finished his apprenticeship as an upholsterer in 1939. Graduated from the School of Fine Art and Crafts in 1944. Operated his own design company with his wife, Nanna Ditzel, from 1946 to 1961.

HONORS> See above.

MATERIALS> Beech
18 x 16^{13}/$_{16}$ x 28^{13}/$_{32}$ / Sh 21^{9}/$_{32}$ in. / 6.6 lbs.
450 x 420 x 710 / Sh 532 mm / 3.0 kg
MANUFACTURER> A/S Kold Savvaerk, Poul Kold

The Ditzels designed many types of children's chairs and this is one of their most popular. The beautiful, stable construction exemplifies the high quality of their work. The rounded top rail is a distinctive feature of one of the best high chair designs in Danish modern furniture.

DESIGNER(S)>	NAME>	YEAR>
NANNA DITZEL / JØRGEN DITZEL	BABY CHAIR	1955

MATERIALS> Beech, Fabric
34¹³/₁₆ x 37 x 37³/₁₆ / Sh 15¹³/₃₂ in. / 37.18 lbs.
870 x 925 x 930 / Sh 385 mm / 16.9 kg
MANUFACTURER> A/S Kold Savvaerk

The large curves of this chair's frame are representative of the round curves characterizing the work of Jørgen and Nanna Ditzel. If Hans J. Wegner's Peacock Chair had a single, solid back construction, it would probably take on the appearance of this chair. In fact, Wegner unveiled a version of his Peacock Chair with a solid back the same year this chair was produced. Although this occurred by chance, one cannot help but notice the striking similarities between these two works by different masters.

DESIGNER(S)>
NANNA DITZEL / JØRGEN DITZEL

NAME>
EASY CHAIR

YEAR>
1953

MATERIALS> Teak, Fabric

$33^{19}/_{32}$ x $26^{3}/_{16}$ x $26^{13}/_{32}$ / Sh $15^{3}/_{16}$ in. / 27.5 lbs.

840 x 655 x 660 / Sh 380 mm / 12.5 kg

MANUFACTURER> A/S Kold Savvaerk, Fredericia Stolefabrik

The key element of the Ditzels' design is the circle. In addition to being round in form, the arms of this chair also have round cross sections. It was out of production for a long time but has been produced by Fredericia Stolefabrik since 1922.

MATERIALS> Cane, Fabric
34 x 32 x 48 / Sh $^{11}/_{16}$ in. / 16.5 lbs.
850 x 800 x 1200 / Sh 17.2 mm / 7.5 kg
MANUFACTURER> R. Wengler, Bonatina (Italy)

Chairs that hang from the ceiling are frequently designed but seldom produced for sale. This chair has been in production from the time of its design more than thirty years ago. The defunct Yamakawa Rattan Co. of Japan once produced it. It is now being produced in Italy.

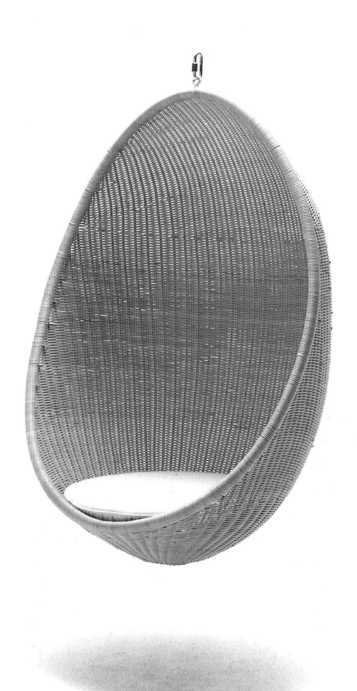

DESIGNER(S)>	NAME>	YEAR>
NANNA DITZEL / JØRGEN DITZEL	SWINGING CHAIR	1959

KRISTIANSOLMERVEDEL

[DESIGNER] **1923–**

KRISTIAN SOLMER VEDEL

Journeyman joiner, 1942. Graduated from the School of Arts, Crafts, and Design, 1946. Studied at the Royal Danish Academy of Fine Arts, Department of Furniture Design, as a Hospitant, 1944–45. Employed by Tove and Edvard Kindt-Larsen 1946–49 and by Palle Suenson 1949–52 and 1953–55. Teacher at the School of Arts, Crafts, and Design, 1953–56. Opened his own office in 1955. Visiting professor of Industrial Design at the East African University, Nairobi, 1969–71, 1975.
HONORS> Lunning Prize, 1962.

MATERIALS> Rosewood, Leather
29 x 25^{13}/$_{32}$ x 24^{19}/$_{32}$ / Sh 14^{13}/$_{32}$ in. / 18.7 lbs.
22 x 22 x 16^{13}/$_{32}$ / Sh 13.72 in. / 13.2 lbs.
725 x 635 x 615 / Sh 360 mm / 8.5 kg
550 x 550 x 410 / Sh 343 mm / 6.0 kg
MANUFACTURER> Søren Willadsen

One of Vedel's best designs, this chair features a soft, loose cushion of leather. The seat, arms, and back are separate pieces. The frame construction differs markedly from that used for ordinary chairs. An armless chair and a highback chair were also designed.

Kristian S. Vedel / Modous easy chair / 1963 / Søren Willadsen

---

DESIGNER(S)>
KRISTIAN SOLMER VEDEL

NAME>
MODOUS EASY CHAIR

YEAR>
1963

POUL**M.VOLTHER**

[DESIGNER] **1923–**

POUL M. VOLTHER

Journeyman joiner. Studied at the School of Arts, Crafts, and Design, Joiner School. Maintains his own office. Teacher at the School of Arts, Crafts, and Design, Department of Furniture Design. Teacher at the architecture school.

MATERIALS> Teak, Fabric
$19^{19}/_{32}$ x 20 x 31 / Sh $17^{3}/_{16}$ in. / 9.9 lbs.
490 x 500 x 775 / Sh 430 mm / 4.5 kg
MANUFACTURER> F. D. B.

This dining chair was designed for the Farmers' Cooperative Association of Denmark. The most distinctive feature of the chair is the construction of the back, consisting of three panels. Though most ladder back–type chairs are characterized by panels that fit between the left and right legs of the chair, the panels of this particular chair extend well beyond the left and right portions of the frame. This feature substantially increases the surface area of the chair's back.

DESIGNER(S)>	NAME>	YEAR>
POUL M. VOLTHER	DINING CHAIR	1951

EJVIND**A.JOHANSSON**

[DESIGNER] **1923–**

EJVIND A. JOHANSSON

Journeyman joiner, 1942. Graduated from the School of Arts, Crafts, and Design, 1949.

MATERIALS> Beech
$17^{3}/_{16}$ x 18 x $30^{13}/_{32}$ / Sh $18^{3}/_{16}$ in. / 11 lbs.
430 x 450 x 790 / Sh 453 mm / 5.0 kg
MANUFACTURER> F. D. B.

This chair, also designed for the Farmers' Cooperative Association, features slits that allow the back to round to fit the contours of the human body. This well-designed, low-cost chair is a good example of the type of furniture sold by the Farmers' Cooperative Association.

DESIGNER(S)>	NAME>	YEAR>
EJVIND A. JOHANSSON	DINING CHAIR	CA. 1957

ELMARMOLTKENIELSEN

[ARCHITECT] **1924–**

KNUDFRIIS

[ARCHITECT] **1926–**

ELMAR MOLTKE NIELSEN

Graduated from the Royal Danish Academy of Fine Arts, School of Architecture. Since 1957 has built hotels, and schools in collaboration with Knud Friis.

HONORS> Wood Prize, 1959. Eckersberg Medal, 1967. Danish Furniture Prize, 1972. Concrete Prize, 1972. Architecture Prize, BDA, Bavaria, 1975. C. F. Hansen Medal, 1987.

KNUD FRIIS

Graduated from the Royal Danish Academy of Fine Arts, School of Architecture, 1950. Professor at the School of Architecture in Århus, 1967–70. Visiting professor at Ball State University, Indiana, 1975. Since 1957, has built hotels and schools with Moltke Nielsen.

HONORS> Wood Prize, 1959. Eckersberg Medal, 1967. Danish Furniture Prize, 1972. Concrete Prize, 1972. Architecture Prize, BDA, Bavaria, 1975. Honorary Fellow of the American Institute of Architects, 1983. C. F. Hansen Medal, 1987.

MATERIALS> Beech
$23^{19}/_{32}$ x $20^{19}/_{32}$ x $30^{13}/_{32}$ / Sh 18 in. / 17.6 lbs.
590 x 515 x 760 / Sh 450 mm / 8.0 kg
MANUFACTURER> Fritz Hansens Eftf.

This chair features flexible construction. The arms can be removed for stacking. A series of these chairs can be connected by joining them with metal fittings. The chair comes in natural or colored finish.

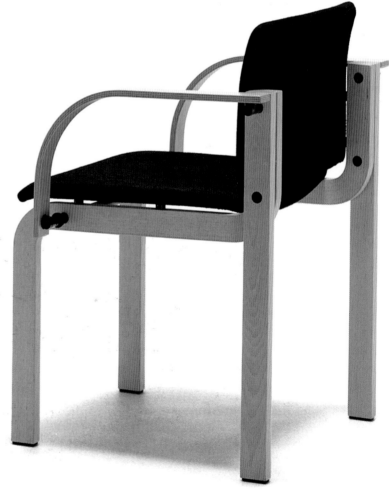

DESIGNER(S)>	NAME>	YEAR>
ELMAR MOLTKE NIELSEN / KNUD FRIIS	FM ARM CHAIR	1985

JØRGEN**HØJ**

[DESIGNER] **1925–**

JØRGEN HØJ

Trained as a smith. Journeyman upholsterer, 1974 (silver medal). Graduated from the School of Arts, Crafts, and Design, 1950. Opened his own design office in 1956, specializing in graphics and interiors.

MATERIALS> Ash, Flag halyard
$26^3/_{16}$ x $31^{19}/_{32}$ x $24^{13}/_{32}$ / Sh $11^3/_{16}$ in. / 13.2 lbs.
655 x 790 x 610 / Sh 280 mm / 6.0 kg
MANUFACTURER> Thorald Madsen, PP Møbler

This is the only chair exhibited by Poul Kjærholm at the Cabinetmakers' Guild Exhibition. Made in collaboration with Jørgen Høj, the chair's extraordinary structure is based on an African native's chair. Very few of them were made.

DESIGNER(S)>	NAME>	YEAR>
JØRGEN HØJ	EASY CHAIR	1952

HENNING**LARSEN**

[PROFESSOR, DESIGNER] **1925–**

HENNING LARSEN

Apprentice carpenter. Graduated from technical school, 1948. Graduated from the Royal Danish Academy of Fine Arts, 1952. Studied and traveled in Britain, United States, Mexico, and South America. Opened his own office in 1956. Teacher at the Royal Danish Academy of Fine Arts from 1959 and professor since 1968. Visiting professor at Yale and Princeton Universities.

HONORS> First prize in the competition for the university in Trondheim, the ministry of foreign affairs in Saudi Arabia, and the Kammergericht in West Berlin. Eckersberg Medal, 1965. Wood Prize, 1984. C. F. Hansen Medal, 1985.

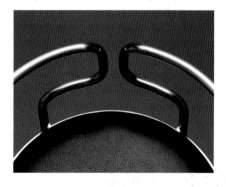

MATERIALS> Steel, Leather
21³/₁₆ x 16¹³/₁₆ x 26¹⁹/₃₂ / Sh 18⁴⁹/₆₄ in. / 14.96 lbs.
530 x 420 x 665 / Sh 469 mm / 6.8 kg
MANUFACTURER> Fritz Hansens Eftf.

This chair design shows the influence of one of Poul Kjærholm's chairs. The one-piece construction of the front leg, half the top rail, and the back leg is unique. This chair is quite comfortable for sitting.

ARNE**VODDER**

[ARCHITECT, DESIGNER] **1926–**

ARNE VODDER

Trained as an architect in Copenhagen. Opened his own office in 1951.
HONORS> Milano Triennale Prize.

MATERIALS> Beech, Leather
$23^{13}/_{16}$ x 20 x $31^{13}/_{32}$ / Sh $19^{3}/_{16}$ in. / 9.9 lbs.
595 x 500 x 785 / Sh 480 mm / 4.5 kg
MANUFACTURER> Sibast Møbler

This chair was introduced in the magazine *MOBILIA* in 1964, where it was called a "handsome chair," implying simple but noble features. The details of the design of its arms and legs are excellent.

DESIGNER(S)>	NAME>	YEAR>
ARNE VODDER	DINING CHAIR	1964

VERNER**PANTON**

[DESIGNER] **1926–**

VERNER PANTON

Odence technical school. Graduated from the Royal Danish Academy of Fine Arts, School of Architecture, 1951. Worked with Arne Jacobsen. Studied abroad 1952–55. Opened his own office in 1955.

HONORS> International Design Award, U.S.A., 1963 and 1968. Rosental Studio Prize, Germany, 1967. PH Prize, 1967. Eurodomus, Italy, 1968. IV Wiener International Mobelsalon honorary prize, 1969. Bundespreis Gute Form, 1972 and 1986. Danish Furniture Prize, 1978. ASID Prize, U.S.A., 1981. Deutsch Auswahl, Stuttgart, 1981, 1982, and 1984.

MATERIALS> Molded glass-fiber shell
$19^{19}/_{32}$ x $22^{13}/_{16}$ x $32^{13}/_{16}$ / Sh $19^{13}/_{16}$ in. / 17.6 lbs.
490 x 570 x 820 / Sh 495 mm / 8.0 kg
MANUFACTURER> Herman Miller (U.S.A.), Vitra (Germany)

This chair made Panton's name famous. It was first produced in the United States by the Herman Miller Co. The design shows the influence of a prototype chair designed by Poul Kjærholm in 1953. The chair is now produced by Vitra Co. in Germany.

DESIGNER(S)>	NAME>	YEAR>
VERNER PANTON	STACKING CHAIR OR PANTON CHAIR	1960

MATERIALS> Steel tube frame, Leather
$20^{13}/_{16}$ x 28 x $29^{19}/_{32}$ / Sh $12^{13}/_{16}$ in. / 11.22 lbs.
520 x 700 x 740 / Sh 320 mm / 5.1 kg
MANUFACTURER> Fritz Hansens Eftf.

Like Arne Jacobsen, Verner Panton is a craftsman who, instead of creating handicraft-type
wooden chairs of typical Danish design, uses
materials such as plastic and metal to create
chairs with a more international look. A fine
example, this chair is leather bound, with a
steel tube frame construction, and it can be
knocked down for storage. When disassembled,
it fits into a small, flat package. A table of similar construction was also created to go with
the chair as a set. A chair of the same design
was created and produced in wood by Fritz
Hansens Eftf.

DESIGNER(S)>
VERNER PANTON

NAME>
BACHELOR CHAIR

YEAR>
1955

JØRGEN**HØVELSKOV**

[DESIGNER] **DATE OF BIRTH AND DEATH UNKNOWN**

MATERIALS> Ash, Flag halyard
42 x 40 x 53³/₁₆ / Sh 15¹³/₁₆ in. / 13.64 lbs.
1050 x 1000 x 1330 / Sh 395 mm / 6.2 kg
MANUFACTURER> Christensen & Larsen Møbelhåndværk

This chair's shape gives it the name Harp Chair. Its three wooden legs have curves like those of an old Viking ship. The legs are joined in the center with a single metal bolt, providing for a knockdown feature. The woven-string back and seat give it the form of sculpture.

DESIGNER(S)>	NAME>		YEAR>
JØRGEN HØVELSKOV	HARP CHAIR OR STRING CHAIR		1968

SIGURD**RESSELL**

[DESIGNER] **DATE OF BIRTH AND DEATH UNKNOWN**

MATERIALS> Oak, Leather
26 x 22^{19}/$_{32}$ x 29^{19}/$_{32}$ / Sh 18^{9}/$_{16}$ in. / 13.2 lbs.
650 x 565 x 740 / Sh 464 mm / 6.0 kg
MANUFACTURER> Niels Vodder

This chair, made in the Niels Vodder workshop,
has a beautiful top rail and is similar to The
Chair designed by Wegner. The top rail is composed of three pieces of wood. The construction demonstrates high standards of design and
craftsmanship.

DESIGNER(S)>	NAME>	YEAR>
SIGURD RESSELL	ARM CHAIR	1959

POUL**KJÆRHOLM**

[PROFESSOR, DESIGNER] **1929–80**

POUL KJÆRHOLM

Poul Kjærholm graduated from the Royal Danish Academy of Fine Arts, Department of Furniture Design, in 1952 and continued at the Academy as an instructor. He was promoted to the position of lecturer in 1959 and was awarded a professorship in 1972. His extraordinary talents were readily apparent from the earliest stages of his career, and he was often referred to as a genius in his field. Traditionally, Danish designers used wood almost exclusively as the primary material for their works. Poul Kjærholm, however, chose steel for his designs. His remarkably delicate and sharp details contrast strikingly with the severity of his lines and proportions. Virtually every aspect of his work, from his selection of materials to the development and harmonization of form, construction, and color, exudes a certain absoluteness, an expression of his discipline and standards. His designs are characterized by the use of cantilever and tension constructions that enable him to create works based on an entirely new furniture design concept. He is well-known for the many masterpieces he created in cooperation with E. Kold Christensen, Co.

HONORS> Grand Prix, Milano Triennale, 1957, 1960. Danish Society of Arts and Crafts, annual prize, 1957. Lunning Prize, 1958. Eckersberg Medal, 1960. Danish Furniture Manufacturers' Association, annual prize, 1972, 1988. ID Prize, 1973.

MATERIALS> Steel, Leather
25³/₁₆ x 26¹³/₁₆ x 28¹³/₃₂ / Sh 13⁷/₈ in. / 27.28 lbs.
630 x 670 x 710 / Sh 347 mm / 12.4 kg
MANUFACTURER> E. Kold Christensen, Fritz Hansens
Eftf.

The design of this chair was influenced by the chair designed by architect Mies van der Rohe. Using flat steel bars as in van der Rohe's Barcelona Chair, Kjærholm came up with a different design solution. This chair, of knock-down construction, has a seat of leather. Another version has a rattan seat.

| DESIGNER(S)> | NAME> | YEAR> |
| POUL KJÆRHOLM | EASY CHAIR, PK-22 | 1955 |

MATERIALS> Steel, Ash, Leather
25^{19}/$_{32}$ x 18 x 26 / Sh 16^{13}/$_{32}$ in.
640 x 450 x 650 / Sh 410 mm
MANUFACTURER> E. Kold Christensen, Fritz Hansens Eftf.

Poul Kjærholm created a total of seven three-legged chair designs throughout his career. This arm chair has been acclaimed for the superb utilization of materials in its design. The horizontal pieces are made of composite ash, the seat is leather, and the frame is steel. No other piece has achieved such a harmonious blend of so many different materials. The chair was designed with a desk.

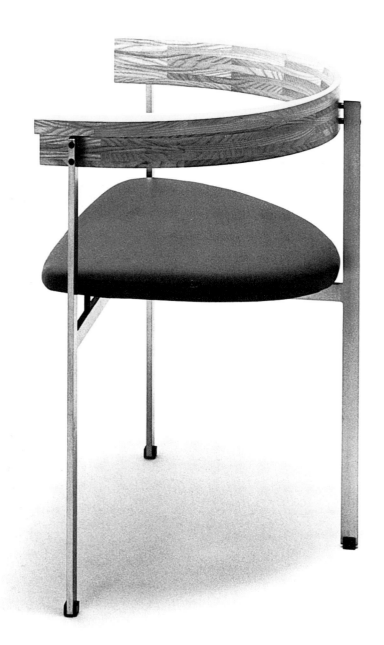

DESIGNER(S)>	NAME>	YEAR>
POUL KJÆRHOLM	ARM CHAIR, PK-11	1957

MATERIALS> Steel, Leather
$22^{13}/_{32}$ x 24 x $29^{19}/_{32}$ / Sh $16^{13}/_{32}$ in.
560 x 600 x 740 / Sh 410 mm
MANUFACTURER> E. Kold Christensen, Fritz Hansens Eftf.

This chair is probably the single best example of a three-legged work with metal fixtures, and the legs are especially beautiful. To enhance the beauty of the legs, the seat was designed so that it appears to be floating above the legs. This masterpiece of design was accompanied by a round, stone table with steel legs. By attaching maple fittings, the diameter of the table can be changed from 56 to 84 inches (140 to 210 cm).

DESIGNER(S)>
POUL KJÆRHOLM

NAME>
DINING CHAIR, PK-9

YEAR>
1960

MATERIALS> Steel, Leather
24 x 18 x 15⁵/₁₆ / Sh 16⁹/₃₂ in. / 16.28 lbs.
600 x 450 x 370 / Sh 383 mm / 7.4 kg
MANUFACTURER> E. Kold Christensen, Fritz Hansens Eftf.

This chair is one of the three most well known Danish folding stool designs. The twisting surfaces of the leg sections give the work its unique and striking beauty. A small ball bearing incorporated in the joint of the leg crossing insures that the chair folds smoothly. Though the term "folding chair" usually denotes cheap, light chairs of simple design and construction, this chair succeeds in establishing a totally new and different image. The seat portion of the chair is leather with two separate pieces fitted together in a double layer to insure that the natural stretching does not adversely affect the chair.

DESIGNER(S)>	NAME>	YEAR>
POUL KJÆRHOLM	FOLDING STOOL, PK-91	1961

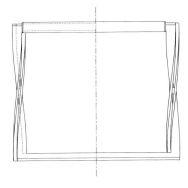

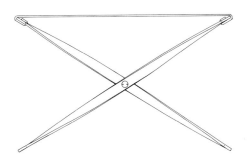

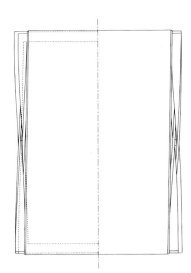

MATERIALS> Steel, Cane
26⁹/₃₂ x 20³¹/₃₂ x 27¹/₈ / Sh 17³/₆₄ in. / 24.2 lbs.
657 x 524 x 678 / Sh 426 mm / 11.0 kg
MANUFACTURER> E. Kold Christensen

Referred to as the elusive masterpiece of Kjærholm's works, this chair features vertical parts that do not come into contact with each other, creating a tension in the suspension that ultimately proved the downfall of the chair as a product and resulted in the discontinuation of production. The chairs that were produced for sale had leather seats and leather-bound arms. Only two chairs were produced as shown here. They are considered custom-made pieces and have been bound in rattan.

Poul Kjærholm / Arm chair / 1980 / Fritz Hansens Eftf., PP Møbler

DESIGNER(S)>
POUL KJÆRHOLM

NAME>
ARM CHAIR, EKC-12 (CUSTOM DESIGN)

YEAR>
1962

186

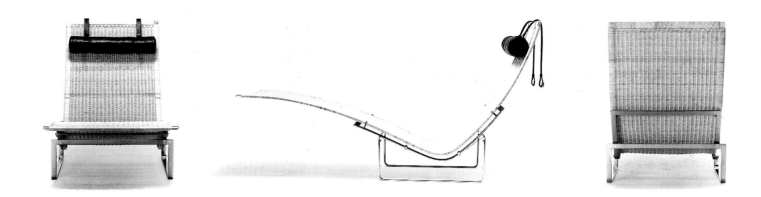

MATERIALS> Stainless steel, Cane, Leather
$26^{13}/_{16}$ x 62 x $34^{13}/_{16}$ / Sh $6^3/_{32}$ in. / 63.8 lbs.
670 x 1550 x 870 / Sh 152 mm / 29.0 kg
MANUFACTURER> E. Kold Christensen, Fritz Hansens
Eftf.

This chair consists of a stainless steel frame balanced on a stainless steel belt set on a U-shaped base. The frame changes position for different uses. The angles of the chair's positions have been graphically illustrated on a beautiful poster offered for sale at the Louisiana Art Museum in Denmark. This chair is designed as well or better than the Cowboy Chair, a flexible-angle lounge chair designed by Le Corbusier, Pierre Jeanneret, and Charlotte Perriand.

DESIGNER(S)>	NAME>	YEAR>
POUL KJÆRHOLM	HAMMOCK CHAIR, PK-24	1965

MATERIALS> Steel, Leather
33 x 30^{13}/$_{32}$ x 25^3/$_{16}$ / Sh 14^9/$_{32}$ in. / 58.3 lbs.
825 x 760 x 880 / Sh 357 mm / 26.5 kg
MANUFACTURER> E. Kold Christensen, Fritz Hansens Eftf.

The first designed with a cantilevered steel frame construction, this chair was designed in 1922 by Harry E. Noland. (A wooden cantilevered frame was designed in 1851.) Many designers then attempted this type of construction. The beautiful curve of the legs and the floating body distinguish this chair.

DESIGNER(S)>
POUL KJÆRHOLM

NAME>
EASY CHAIR, PK-20

YEAR>
1967

188

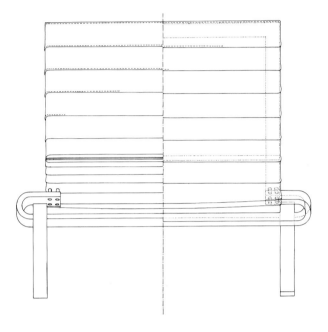

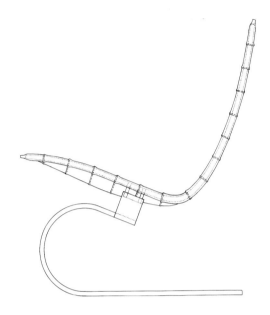

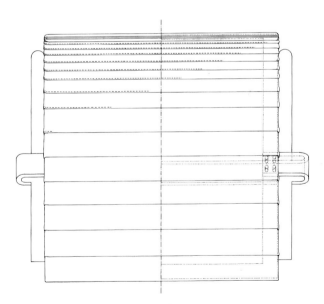

MATERIALS> Maple, Leather
28¹³/₃₂ x 28 x 28¹³/₃₂ / Sh 13¹⁹/₃₂ in. / 25.08 lbs.
710 x 700 x 710 / Sh 340 mm / 11.4 kg
MANUFACTURER> E. Kold Christensen, PP Møbler

This chair is an adaptation of the chair designed in 1965 for the John F. Kennedy Center in the United States. About this time, Kjærholm started to use wood for his chairs. Previously, he had used mainly inorganic materials such as stone, steel, and glass. This chair has inverted U-shaped legs and a cantilevered construction cushioned by a rubber joint.

| DESIGNER(S)> | NAME> | YEAR> |
| POUL KJÆRHOLM | EASY CHAIR, EKC-27 | 1971 |

MATERIALS> Steel, Leather
24³/₁₆ x 20¹⁹/₃₂ x 30³/₁₆ / Sh 16¹⁷/₃₂ in. / 42.24 lbs.
605 x 515 x 755 / Sh 413 mm / 19.2 kg
MANUFACTURER> E. Kold Christensen

This design shows the strong influence of Mies van der Rohe's Bruno Chair, a cantilevered chair. Its distinctive feature is the way the seat and legs are joined using small screws rather than cross pieces. This beautiful chair's weakness is lateral motion. The seat appears to be floating in midair, giving the chair a sculptured appearance. Unfortunately the beauty was not matched by function. The chair is no longer in production.

DESIGNER(S)>
POUL KJÆRHOLM

NAME>
CANTILEVERED ARM CHAIR, EKC-13

YEAR>
1974

MATERIALS> Maple
24 x 22^{13}/$_{32}$ (8^{19}/$_{32}$) x 23^{13}/$_{32}$ / Sh 8^{13}/$_{32}$ in.
600 x 560 (215) x 585 / Sh 210 mm
MANUFACTURER> PP Møbler

This chair was designed for the concert hall of the Louisiana Museum of Modern Art, north of Copenhagen. The seat and back are woven of thinly sliced maple and the frame is also maple. The seat is cantilevered and turned upright by a pivot. Grouped in the concert hall, these chairs show beautiful harmony and rhythm.

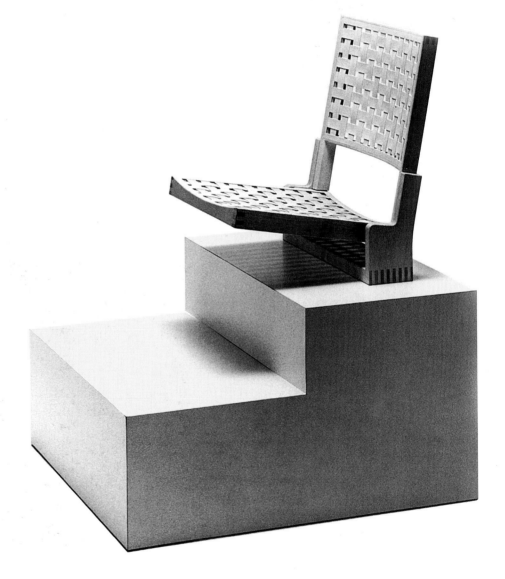

Poul Kjærholm / Theater chair / 1979 / PP Møbler

DESIGNER(S)>
POUL KJÆRHOLM

NAME>
LOUISIANA CHAIR

YEAR>
1976

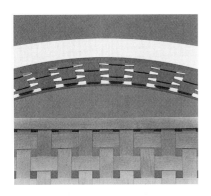

MATERIALS> Maple
22 x 17¹³/₁₆ x 28¹³/₁₆ / Sh 16¹⁹/₃₂ in. / 10.12 lbs.
550 x 445 x 720 / Sh 415 mm / 4.6 kg
MANUFACTURER> PP Møbler

This is an adaptation of the Louisiana Chair and uses the same materials. The back of the chair can be changed. An arm chair was designed at the same time. The chair is in production at PP Møbler Co.

Poul Kjærholm / Easy chair / 1976 / PP Møbler

OLE**GJERLØV-KNUDSEN**

[DESIGNER] **1930–**

OLE GJERLØV-KNUDSEN

Apprenticeship completed under Ludvig Pontoppidan, 1952. Graduated from the School of Arts, Crafts, and Design, Department of Furniture Design, 1955. Studied at the Royal Danish Academy of Fine Arts, Department of Furniture Design. Worked with architect Kay Korbing, 1955–57 and 1960–62. Worked with Vilhelm Lauritzen, 1957–60. Office association with architect Torben Lind since 1962. Teacher at the School of Arts, Crafts, and Design, Department of Furniture Design since 1962. Rector of School of Arts, Crafts, and Design since 1967. Member of the Danish Design Council and Industrial Designers Denmark since 1977.

MATERIALS> Ash, Canvas, Flag halyard
28^{13}/$_{16}$ x 36 x 33 / Sh 12 in. / 9.46 lbs.
720 x 900 x 825 / Sh 300 mm / 4.3 kg
MANUFACTURER> Cado

The legs of this chair are connected by tightly twisted rope, which provides tension and can be used to adjust the frame. The construction is simple. The name comes from the chair's resemblance to a saw. Gjerløv-Knudsen designed a daybed using the same construction, which is easy to separate and knock down.

DESIGNER(S)>
OLE GJERLØV-KNUDSEN

NAME>
SAW CHAIR

YEAR>
1966

194

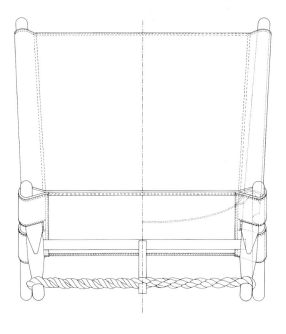

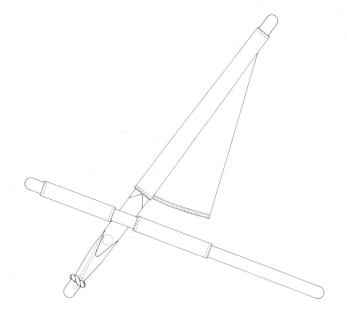

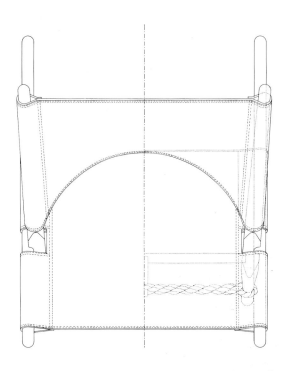

PREBEN**FABRICIUS**

[DESIGNER] **1931–84**

JØRGEN**KASTHOLM**

[DESIGNER] **1938–**

PREBEN FABRICIUS

Served his apprenticeship under Niels Vodder in 1952. Graduated from the School of Interior Design in 1957. Presently teaches at the School of Interior Design. Partnership with Jørgen Kastholm from 1962 to 1970.
HONORS> Illum Prize, 1969. First prize in Good Form, 1969.

JØRGEN KASTHOLM

Studied as a smith at father's workshop, 1953. Graduated from the School of Interior Design, 1958. Graduated from Graphic High School, 1959. Opened his own office in 1960.
HONORS> Illum Prize, 1968. Ringling Museum Award (U.S.A.), 1969. First prize in Good Form, 1969. Good industrial form, 1972, 1974, 1976. Stuttgart Design Center, first prize, 1972, 1977. Grand Prix, Modern Art Museum, Brazil, 1973.

MATERIALS> Steel, Leather
$32^{13}/_{16}$ x $23^{13}/_{16}$ x 27 / Sh 14 in. / 33 lbs.
820 x 595 x 675 / Sh 350 mm / 15.0 kg
MANUFACTURER> Ivan Schlecter

This chair became the topic of conversation when it was shown to the public at the Decorative Art Museum in Paris. Its unique, one-leg design and the beautifully formed shell seat are reminiscent of a tractor seat. The form has high stability. The curved sharp form of the leg resembles a curved Turkish sword, called a scimitar, giving it its name.

DESIGNER(S)>
PREBEN FABRICIUS / JØRGEN KASTHOLM

NAME>
SCIMITAR CHAIR

YEAR>
1962

196

MATERIALS> Steel, Leather
30 x 34^{13}/$_{16}$ x 28^{13}/$_{32}$ / Sh 18^{13}/$_{16}$ in. / 46.2 lbs.
750 x 870 x 710 / Sh 470 mm / 21.0 kg
MANUFACTURER> Bo-EX

The companies Alfred Kill of Germany and Bo-EX of Denmark have produced countless works in cooperation. This particular work is currently produced and sold by Bo-EX. The cantilevered easy chair resembles Kjærholm's work. Its distinctive characteristic is the skillful use of the steel frame.

DESIGNER(S)>
PREBEN FABRICIUS / JØRGEN KASTHOLM

NAME>
EASY CHAIR

YEAR>
CA. 1970

RUD**THYGESEN**

[DESIGNER] **1932–**

JOHNNY**SØRENSEN**

[DESIGNER] **1944–**

RUD THYGESEN

Commercial education, 1953. Graduated from the School of Arts, Crafts, and Design, 1966. Opened his own office with Johnny Sørensen in 1966. Member of the Ministry of Education's committee on training for craftsmen.
HONORS> First Prize, Cabinetmakers' Guild furniture competition, 1968. Danmarks National Bank's Anniversary Foundation of 1968, 1969, 1975. Danish Furniture Manufacturer's Association honorary prize, 1971. Danish Furniture Prize, 1978. Institute of Business Designers' Award, 1978.

JOHNNY SØRENSEN

Journeyman carpenter (silver medal), 1963, Helsingor shipyards. Graduated from the School of Arts, Crafts, and Design, 1967. Opened his own office with Rud Thygesen in 1966.
HONORS> First prize, Cabinetmakers' Guild anniversary exhibition, 1966. First prize, Cabinetmakers' Guild furniture competition, 1968. Danmarks National Bank's Anniversary Foundation of 1968, 1969, 1975. Danish Furniture Manufacturer's Association honorary prize, 1971. Danish Furniture Prize, 1978. Institute of Business Designers' Award, 1978.

MATERIALS> Oak, Cane
$24^{13}/_{32}$ x 28 x 28 / Sh $13^{13}/_{32}$ in. / 11.66 lbs.
610 x 700 x 700 / Sh 335 mm / 5.3 kg
MANUFACTURER> Botium

Named the King's Chair because it was presented to Denmark's King Frederik on his birthday, this chair received first prize at the 1969 Cabinetmakers' Guild Exposition. The prototype was made at the Christensen & Larsen workshop. A two-person chair was also designed.

DESIGNER(S)>	NAME>	YEAR>
RUD THYGESEN / JOHNNY SØRENSEN	**KING'S CHAIR**	1968

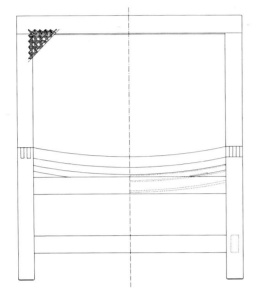

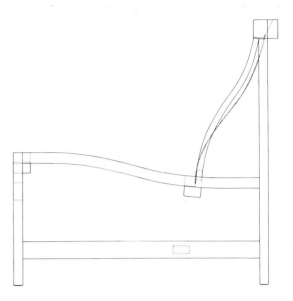

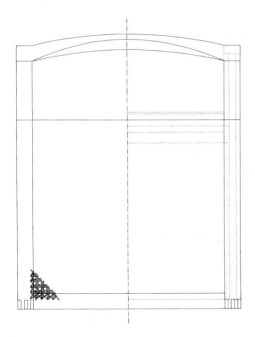

MATERIALS> Beech, Leather
$25^{3}/_{16}$ x 19 x 28 / Sh $18^{13}/_{16}$ in. / 14.3 lbs.
630 x 475 x 700 / Sh 470 mm / 6.5 kg
MANUFACTURER> Magnus Olesen

The distinctive feature of this chair is its arm design. What appears to be a simple laminate wood arm is curved, thick, laminated wood. The three legs, also made of laminated wood, are black or white. Unfortunately, this chair was recently taken out of production.

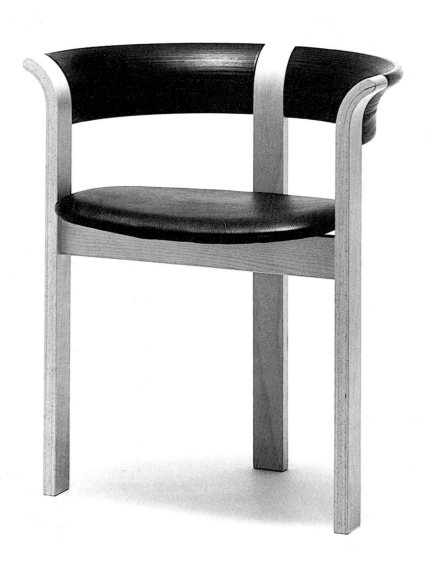

DESIGNER(S)>	NAME>	YEAR>
RUD THYGESEN / JOHNNY SØRENSEN	ARM CHAIR № 4551	1974

MATERIALS> Beech
21¹⁹/₃₂ x 18³/₁₆ x 26¹³/₁₆ / Sh 16¹³/₃₂ in. / 7.7 lbs.
540 x 455 x 670 / Sh 410 mm / 3.5 kg
MANUFACTURER> Magnus Olesen A/S

The idea of the chair's construction came from the cross section of the beech wood used, in particular where the branch joins the trunk. The legs are joined to the seat by wedging and gluing them in. The idea was to use no nails or screws and to use a material of low water content so that after the gluing the wood would expand, making an extremely tight joint. This chair received the Japanese Good Design Prize in 1990.

Rud Thygesen, Johnny Sørensen / High stool / 1981 / Magnus Olesen A/S

DESIGNER(S)>
RUD THYGESEN / JOHNNY SØRENSEN

NAME>
ARM CHAIR

YEAR>
1981

201

STEEN**ØSTERGAARD**

[DESIGNER] **1935–**

STEEN ØSTERGAARD

Journeyman joiner (silver medal), 1957. Graduated from the School of Arts, Crafts, and Design, 1960. Employed by Finn Juhl, 1962–65. Opened his own office in 1965. Head of product development, Poul Cadovius, 1970–74. Examiner, School of Interior Design. HONORS> First prize Saddlemaker's and Upholsterers' Guild anniversary competition, 1960. First prize, international furniture competition in Cantu, Italy, 1963. Prizes from Copenhagen Cabinetmakers' Guild, 1964 and 1965.

MATERIALS> Polyamide, Fabric
$20^{13}/_{16}$ x $21^{13}/_{32}$ x $30^{3}/_{16}$ / Sh 18 in. / 9.9 lbs.
520 x 545 x 755 / Sh 450 mm / 4.5 kg
MANUFACTURER> Poul Cadovius, Cado

This stacking chair is similar to Kjærholm's chair and Panton's chair. The large hole in the legs makes the chair lighter and saves on material costs. Compared to the works of Panton, the various elements of this chair are rather thin. Curves have been generously used in order to strengthen and reinforce the overall design. An arm chair and a highback chair were also designed.

Steen Østergaard / Arm chair / 1968 / Cado

DESIGNER(S)>	NAME>	YEAR>
STEEN ØSTERGAARD	STACKING CHAIR	1968

JENS**NIELSEN**

[ARCHITECT] **1937–93**

JENS NIELSEN

Graduated from high school in 1956. Studied at the University of Copenhagen from 1956 to 1957. Studied at the School of Architecture at the Art Academy from 1958 to 1964. Graduated in 1966 having specialized in the field of industrial design. Published several articles about architecture and industrial design in Danish and foreign newspapers and technical periodicals. Manager for design exhibitions at home and abroad. Member of the Danish Design Group in the Council of Industry from 1975 to 1977. Member of the Executive Committee of the Danish Council of Design from 1977.

MATERIALS> Beech
$21^{19}/_{32}$ x $29^{19}/_{32}$ x 28 / Sh $14^{17}/_{32}$ in. / 22 lbs.
540 x 740 x 700 / Sh 363 mm / 10.0 kg
MANUFACTURER> Westnofa (Norway)

Simply constructed of two curved pieces of laminated wood joined together, this chair displays a beautiful shape and an innovative design concept. The chair received a prize in an industrial design competition for use of plywood. It is being produced in Norway by Westnofa, but it has never been produced in Denmark.

DESIGNER(S)>	NAME>	YEAR>
JENS NIELSEN	LAMINEX CHAIR	1966

NIELS-JØRGEN**HAUGESEN**

[DESIGNER] **1936–**

NIELS-JØRGEN HAUGESEN

Journeyman joiner, 1956. Graduated from the School of Arts, Crafts, and Design, 1961. Employed by Arne Jacobsen, 1966–71. Teacher of furniture design at the School of Arts, Crafts, and Design. Opened his own office in 1971 and has collaborated with textile designer Gunvor Haugesen since 1980.

HONORS> First prize, Swedish Forestry Society competition, 1963. Second prize, Danish Forestry Society competition, 1965. Second Prize, Swedish furniture industry, Nordic competition, 1965. Danmarks National Bank's Anniversary Foundation of 1968, 1969, and 1987. Danish State Art Foundation, 1982 and 1987. First prize, Danish Forestry Society competition, 1989.

MATERIALS> Steel
$19^{13}/_{16}$ x $19^{13}/_{32}$ x $30^{13}/_{16}$ / Sh $17^{13}/_{16}$ in. / 11 lbs.
495 x 485 x 770 / Sh 445 mm / 5.0 kg
MANUFACTURER> Hybodon A/S

This stacking chair is made of steel rods and punched metal. The X-shaped brace under the seat is the strong point of this design. Haugesen often used steel rods or wire ropes in his designs. The materials give a sharp impression to his furniture.

DESIGNER(S)>	NAME>	YEAR>
NIELS-JØRGEN HAUGESEN	X-LINE CHAIR	1977

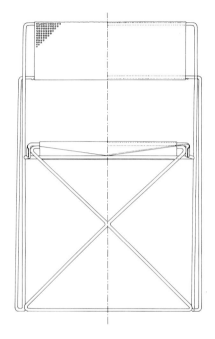

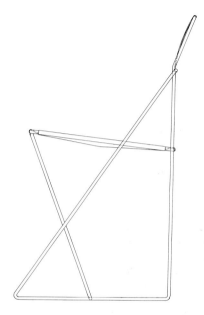

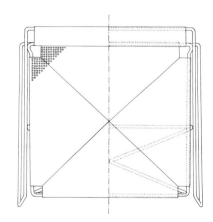

BERNT**PETERSEN**

[DESIGNER] **1937–**

BERNT PETERSEN

Journeyman joiner, silver medal, 1957. Graduated from the School of Arts, Crafts, and Design, 1960. Opened his own office in 1963. Teacher, School of Arts, Crafts, and Design, 1973–77. Lecturer, Royal Danish Academy of Fine Arts, Department of Furniture Design, 1977–85. Supervised and collaborated on interior furnishings for theaters, a congress center, libraries, and other civic buildings in Denmark and abroad.

HONORS> First prize, Danish Forestry competition, 1964. Illum Prize, 1966. First prize, Danish Furniture Manufacturers' Association, 1969. Danish Society of Arts and Crafts annual prize, 1970. Danmarks National Bank's Anniversary Foundation of 1968, 1972. Danish State Art Foundation, 1972, 1976, 1987. Danish Furniture Prize, 1977. Second prize, Danish Forestry competition, 1988. Various Danish grants.

MATERIALS> Ash, Cane
22 x 22 x 14^{13}/$_{32}$ / Sh 16 in. / 5.5 lbs.
550 x 550 x 360 / Sh 400 mm / 2.5 kg
MANUFACTURER> Worts Møbelsnedkeri

The design of this chair was created while Petersen was studying at the Royal Danish Academy of Fine Arts and was submitted as his graduation project. The seat was woven of cotton belting in the original design but here it is woven of cane. The frame looks very thin but is actually of strong construction. The carved legs soften the hardness of this model, and the ends of the legs are as elegantly designed as the feet of a cat. This chair is still in production.

MATERIALS> Mahogany, Cane, Leather
29 x 25^{13}/$_{32}$ x 14^{13}/$_{32}$ / Sh 18^{13}/$_{16}$ in. / 27.72 lbs.
725 x 635 x 360 / Sh 470 mm / 12.6 kg
MANUFACTURER> Worts Møbelsnedkeri

This design uses the same principle seen in the chairs designed by Kaare Klint and Hans J. Wegner, adaptations of old English chairs of the eighteenth century. It is representative of the furniture designs influenced by Klint during his active period.

DESIGNER(S)>	NAME>	YEAR>
BERNT PETERSEN	ARM CHAIR	1962

MATERIALS> Mahogany, Cane
$18^{13}/_{32}$ x $19^{3}/_{16}$ x $28^{13}/_{16}$ / Sh $17^{19}/_{32}$ in. / 9.24 lbs.
460 x 480 x 720 / Sh 440 mm / 4.2 kg
MANUFACTURER> Worts Møbelsnedkeri

This chair is a variation of the piece shown on page 207 and has had a back added to the original work. Considering the history of chair development in England, this armless chair is classified as a back stool, designed so that the person sitting on the stool can lean backwards and have support. The design is Bernt Petersen's contribution to the further development of stool design and can be considered one of his better works.

DESIGNER(S)>	NAME>	YEAR>
BERNT PETERSEN	DINING CHAIR	1963

JØRGEN**GAMMELGAARD**

[PROFESSOR, DESIGNER] **1938–92**

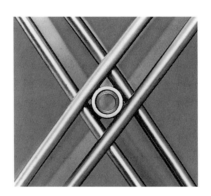

JØRGEN GAMMELGAARD

Journeyman joiner (silver medal) 1957, under C. F. Hansen. Employed by A. J. Iversen's Furniture workshop, 1957–59. The School of Arts, Crafts, and Design, Department of Furniture Design, 1959–62. Auditor, the Royal Danish Academy of Fine Arts, Department of Furniture Design, 1962–64. Consultant for U.N. in Polynesia, 1965–67. Employed by Arne Jacobsen, Jørgen Bo, Bernt, 1968–71. Opened his own office in 1973. Professor, the Royal Danish Academy of Fine Arts, Department of Furniture Design.

HONORS> Prizes in Cabinetmakers' Guild competitions. Danish Furniture Prize, 1971. The Crafts Council's annual prize, 1987. The Danish Design Council's annual prize, 1987.

MATERIALS> Steel, Leather
$22^{13}/_{16}$ x $18^{13}/_{32}$ x $16^{13}/_{32}$ / Sh $16^{19}/_{32}$ in. / 12.1 lbs.
570 x 460 x 410 / Sh 415 mm / 5.5 kg
MANUFACTURER> Design Forum

This work, designed by Gammelgaard, is one of the three famous folding stools of Danish design. (The others are designed by Klint and Kjærholm.) Made of steel rods, each of its legs is beautifully curved. In Denmark, a designer is recognized as a master in accordance with his ability to produce stools and chairs of three-legged or folding design.

DESIGNER(S)>	NAME>	YEAR>
JØRGEN GAMMELGAARD	FOLDING STOOL	1970

MATERIALS> Beech, Fabric
23 x 36³/₁₆ x 41 / Sh 19³/₃₂ in. / 33.44 lbs.
575 x 905 x 1025 / Sh 477 mm / 15.2 kg
MANUFACTURER> Erik Jørgensen

This rocking chair is similar to the chair designed by Josef Hoffmann in Austria, the side view of which also shows oval legs. The knockdown construction of this chair provides for easy transport.

DESIGNER(S)>
JØRGEN GAMMELGAARD

NAME>
ROCKING CHAIR

YEAR>
1982

TAGE**POULSEN**

[DESIGNER] **1940–**

TAGE POULSEN

Journeyman joiner, 1959. Graduated from the School of Arts, Crafts, and Design, 1964. Opened his own office and workshop in 1965. HONORS> Furniture Prize, 1974.

MATERIALS> Oak, Leather
$20^{13}/_{16}$ x $21^{13}/_{16}$ x $33^{3}/_{32}$ / Sh $18^{31}/_{64}$ in. / 16.72 lbs.
520 x 545 x 827 / Sh 462 mm / 7.6 kg
MANUFACTURER> Berg Furniture

The English Chippendale chair was redesigned by Klint and unveiled as the Red Chair. The material used for the seat and back is sixteenth-inch-thick water buffalo leather, usually referred to as mammoth leather. Poulsen designed a similar sofa and dining chair.

Tage Poulsen / Dining chair / 1981 / Berg Furniture

DESIGNER(S)>	NAME>	YEAR>
TAGE POULSEN	ARM CHAIR	1981

ERIK**MAGNUSSEN**

[DESIGNER] **1940–**

ERIK MAGNUSSEN

Studied pottery and glass. Graduated from the
School of Arts, Crafts, and Design, Department
of Ceramics, 1960. Opened his own office in
1960. Worked for Bing & Grondahls Porcelain
workshop since 1962.

HONORS> Lunning Prize, 1967. ID Prize, 1972.
Furniture Prize, 1975.

MATERIALS> Steel, Canvas
19¹⁹/₃₂ x 23³/₆₄ x 29³/₁₆ / Sh 19¹³/₃₂ in. / 10.56 lbs.
490 x 576 x 730 / Sh 485 mm / 4.8 kg
MANUFACTURER> Toben Orskov & Co.

Erik Magnussen designed both furniture and
tableware. This folding chair is similar to the
chair designed by architect Gerrit Thomas
Rietveld in Holland in 1933. Instead of a folding chair, however, he used steel pipes in the
back. Magnussen also designed a similar chair
with a wide back.

DESIGNER(S)>	NAME>	YEAR>
ERIK MAGNUSSEN	FOLDING CHAIR	1968

ERIK**KROGH**

[DESIGNER] **1942–**

 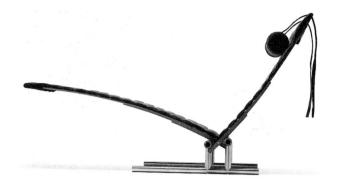 

ERIK KROGH

Journeyman joiner, 1962. Graduated from the School of Arts, Crafts, and Design, Department of Furniture Design, 1965. Auditor at the Royal Danish Academy of Fine Arts, Department of Furniture Design, 1965–69. Teacher at the School of Arts, Crafts, and Design since 1968. Author of articles on design in various newspapers and trade journals. Opened his own office in 1979.

HONORS> Architecture Prize, 1983. Danish Furniture Prize, 1984. Eckersberg Medal, 1988. Grant from the Danish State Art Foundation and Danmarks National Bank's Anniversary Foundation, 1968.

MATERIALS> Beech, Steel, Leather
25³/₁₆ x 58¹³/₁₆ x 33¹⁹/₃₂ / Sh 7³/₁₆–18¹³/₃₂ in. / 44 lbs.
630 x 1470 x 840 / Sh 180–460 mm / 20.0 kg
MANUFACTURER> Arta Form

Reminiscent of the Hammock Chair designed by Poul Kjærholm, the construction is cantilevered from the point where the seat and back meet. The seat is thinner toward the edge and the body slits form the cushion. The knockdown construction demonstrates that furniture can be designed for easy transport. Krogh has a table design using the same type of legs.

DESIGNER(S)>	NAME>	YEAR>
ERIK KROGH	FOLDING LOUNGE CHAIR	1982

EBBE**GEHL**

[DESIGNER] **1942–**

SØREN**NISSEN**

[DESIGNER] **1944–**

EBBE GEHL

Journeyman joiner (silver medal), Rud. Rasmussens Snedkerier, 1959–63. Studied at the School of Arts, Crafts, and Design, Department of Furniture Design, 1963–69. Employed by Nanna Ditzel, 1966–67. Instructor in furniture design at Edinburgh College of Art, 1967–69. Opened his own office with architect Søren Nissen in 1970. HONORS> Prize in Paustian's furniture competition, 1969. Various Danish grants.

SØREN NISSEN

Journeyman's certificate from Rudolf Rasmussen Cabinetmaker's Workshop in 1965 (bronze medal). Graduated from the School of Fine Art and Crafts in 1968. Worked in partnership with Ebbe Gehl from 1970. Danish Pinewood Furniture in Berlin in 1975. The SCAN-Exhibition in Washington in 1976. HONORS> Received the Frederik Borup Grant and grant awarded by the Foundation of Glass Tradesman Johan Franz Ronge. Aage Lichtinger Grant (twice).

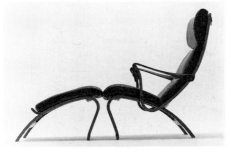

MATERIALS> Teak, Leather
28 x 35^{13}/$_{32}$ x 37^{13}/$_{32}$ / Sh 16^{31}/$_{64}$ in. / 22 lbs.
22 x 25^{19}/$_{32}$ x 15^{3}/$_{16}$ / Sh 15^{31}/$_{64}$ in. / 9.9 lbs.
700 x 885 x 935 / Sh 412 mm / 10.0 kg
550 x 640 x 380 / Sh 387 mm / 4.5 kg
MANUFACTURER> Jeki A/S

Swedish artist Bruno Matoson's Pernila chair series is well known as a masterpiece and noted for its comfort. The lines of the Pernila chairs were taken from the human body at rest. Probably designed with the same factors of comfort in mind, this Clipper easy chair features knockdown construction, making it easy and inexpensive to ship. The construction also allows the chair to be easily stored when not in use.

DESIGNER(S)>	NAME>	YEAR>
EBBE GEHL / SØREN NISSEN	CLIPPER EASY CHAIR	1978

ROALDSTEENHANSEN

[DESIGNER] **1942–**

ROALD STEEN HANSEN

Journeyman joiner (silver medal), 1962. Graduated from the School of Arts, Crafts, and Design, 1967. Graduated from the Royal Danish Academy of Fine Arts, Department of Furniture Design, 1972. Grant to attend the Danish Academy of Science and Art in Rome, 1974–76. Graduate course in industrial design 1982–83. Employed by Arne Jacobsen, 1967–74, and Henning Larsen, 1980–81. Teacher of furniture design at the School of Interior Design.

HONORS> Danish Furniture Prize, 1976. ASID Design Award, 1984. Many grants.

MATERIALS> Beech
$22^{9}/_{32}$ x $28^{3}/_{16}$ x $26^{11}/_{16}$ / Sh $13^{19}/_{32}$ in. / 18.92 lbs.
557 x 705 x 667 / Sh 340 mm / 8.6 kg
MANUFACTURER> Bjarne Bo Andersen

Viewed from the side, the silhouette of this chair is reminiscent of the cantilevered chair designed by Mies van der Rohe. Copies of this beautiful laminated wood chair have been purchased by the Museum of Modern Art in New York City and the Arts and Crafts Museum in Copenhagen for their permanent collections, yet it has never been put into mass production. The outstanding coat-hanger design of this piece has established it as a masterpiece with historic importance and scope.

DESIGNER(S)>	NAME>	YEAR>
ROALD STEEN HANSEN	CANTILEVERED CHAIR (PROTOTYPE)	1975

TORBEN**SKOV**

[DESIGNER] **1947–**

TORBEN SKOV

Graduated from the School of Graphic Design, 1970. Opened his own office in 1971.
HONORS> Silver Medal, Asahikawa International Furniture Competition, 1990.

MATERIALS> Beech
$22^{13}/_{32}$ x $37^{3}/_{16}$ x $43^{3}/_{16}$ / Sh $18^{13}/_{16}$ in. / 24.2 lbs.
560 x 930 x 1080 / Sh 472 mm / 11.0 kg
MANUFACTURER> Norkisk Anders-Eksport

This chair received the silver prize at the 1990 Asahikawa International Furniture Competition. The rocking chair was first designed by Thonet in Austria 130 years ago and many designers have since created their own variations. This chair has excellent construction and a simple, contemporary design.

DESIGNER(S)>	NAME>	YEAR>
TORBEN SKOV	ROCKING CHAIR	1990

AFTERWORD

I was born and raised in a rural area of Kochi Prefecture on the island of Shikoku. We did not have chairs of any sort, because Western-style furniture was rare in Japan before WWII. Even my nursery school did not have chairs during the post-war years. I remember hearing my nursery school teacher talk about sitting directly on the wooden floors. I never sat in a chair until about 1952 when I entered elementary school. Anyone who remembers that time will understand my feelings of nostalgia for that rough, little wooden chair made of square timbers and a wooden board.

A few years later I finally got my very own chair when my family purchased a wooden study desk and chair at the furniture store in our town. The chair even had a spring-cushioned seat covered with cloth. That chair and I were together until I graduated from high school ten years later.

When I went away to college, I got to pick new chairs for my little apartment. I chose a set with a table and three chairs designed by Motoi Yoshihara (1960) and sold by Hida Sangyo Co. The chair design, with its European form and curving wood frame, was awarded the "AG Mark" for good design in 1966 and was popular for a long time thereafter.

Next, I acquired a Windsor-style rocking chair. Imagine my four-and-a-half tatami mat room with my desk, little table, bed, bookcase, and four chairs! They completely filled the space, leaving no room for me.

The history of chairs in the Japanese lifestyle, like my personal history with chairs, only goes back only forty years or so. On the other hand, the history of chairs in the West extends through layer upon layer of history from ancient Egypt, through Roman times to Byzantium and the Renaissance. Relatively speaking, the bentwood furniture by Michel Thonet in the 1850s spread throughout Europe and America in the blink of an eye, in sharp contrast to the situation in Japan. After the war, Western-style furniture was brought to Japan by the occupying forces and took root as strongly as the principles of democracy.

As Western-style furniture spread, Japanese designers copied designs from countries with a long tradition of furniture design. Little by little, Japanese style and craftsmanship began to stand on their own. This process was notably influenced by the traditions of Northern Europe, especially Denmark, where the craftsmanship and the handling of materials had much in common with traditional Japanese technical arts. This may be the reason for the surprising degree to which products from Northern Europe, and especially Denmark, have been adapted to Japanese space.

Even though I am Japanese, my fascination with Danish furniture seems natural. My interest in chairs goes back twenty-six years to when I graduated from university and began working in the advertising department of a department store. Even before that, my father liked furniture and often took me along when we went to visit imported furniture stores in Osaka. At that time, my allowance was about ¥10,000 per month, but on one visit to the stores my father and I frequented, I saw an armchair by Alvar Aalto, who was then unknown to me, and a chair by George Nakashima on sale for ¥30,000 each. I think that my astonishment at that time opened the door to my interest in chairs. After I started working at the department store, I purchased a chair that cost ten times my salary, a Le Corbusier ALC-4 series chaise launching me into the world of chairs.

Initially I was happy just to acquire famous chairs and masterworks, but I began to have questions and decided to take up chairs as a subject of research. With Ms. Kinuko Seo, I established a private research center office called CHAIRs (our logo was designed by Mr. Shuuji Abe) and our research continues to this day. This research can be divided into six categories.

1. Collecting information relating to chairs, including literature, written illustration records, catalogues, and videotapes.

2. Preparing files listing chairs, similar to Japanese family registers, for individual chairs on the basis of the literature.

3. Collecting representative chairs by various craftspeople and designers, from the bentwood chairs of Thonet (1850s) up to the present time. This collection is for the purpose of research, not merely for the sake of collecting.

4. Preparing a photographic library of images of these chairs from all four sides.

5. Preparing and collecting full-size chair plans.

6. Breaking down and illustrating the year-by-year evolution of chair designs by comparing early and later models, from various master builders and furniture designers.

Because of my research, my chair collecting has always been just one-sixth of my research, and I regret that the collection has been the only focus for discussion.

In any event, I would not still be involved in this research if it weren't for Yoshio Hayashi, who was responsible for the photography in this publication. For the past twelve years, and especially during the ten years since before my move to Hokkaido, he has spent his Sundays and holidays photographing these chairs. As I mentioned, each time, the photographs were shot under identical lighting conditions from four directions: front, back, side, and at an angle. Although this may not be a very interesting subject for a photographer, he has taken his pictures without a word of complaint—and always as a volunteer. Mr. Hayashi also introduced me to Mr. Hajime Kirihara, who provided us with the use of his studio without charge over a long period of time and whose staff generously provided us with much help.

Subsequently, other friends of mine did me the favor of lending me the use of their land for the construction of a studio-cum-warehouse. The photography sessions here were unforgettable. On a day when we'd have a session, I would rise at about 5:00 AM and travel two and a half hours to the studio, where we would take pictures until dusk. In the winter, we'd wade through twelve inches of snow to the studio and take pictures in a room where the temperature was quite literally freezing. On the other hand, in the summer, we'd be in a 104°-plus steam bath taking our pictures. Looking back, I have surprisingly good memories of those sessions! This book would never have come into being without Mr. Hayashi's assistance on these photographs.

I am also deeply indebted to Mr. Minoru Nagahara and Ms. Takako Moriya, of the Interior Center Co., Ltd., for their assistance after the collection was moved to Hokkaido.

I must also thank Messrs. Tom and Soren Matts for their cooperation in the collection of chairs for research; without their help I could never have done it. They understood my ideas and became my eyes, ears, and legs in the quest for rare works. I cannot find words to express my appreciation to them. In Japan, with the assistance and understanding of the staff from various imported furniture emporia, I was able to purchase chairs at special prices and was given generous payment terms. Many people also helped us gather information; these furniture designers and master builders, who a decade ago didn't even know us, generously worked with us: Finn Juhl (deceased), Hans J. Wegner, Grete Jalk, Bernt Petersen, Rud Thygesen, Johnny Sørensen, Jørgen Gammelgaard (deceased), Erik Krogh. We had an enjoyable but anxious time with the head of the Denmark Design Center, Mr. Jens Bernsen, who offered assistance at a busy time. And with that refreshed feeling that comes from being really touched, our many thanks to the many companies and studios who trusted us and allowed us to tour their workshops and studios: Fritz Hansens Co., PP Møbler Co., Peter Iepsen Co., Geterma Co., Carl Hansen Co., Fredricia Co., Magnus Olsen Co., Rudolf Rasmussen Co., Soren Horn & Niels Roth Andersen Studio, as well as companies and studios which have since disappeared, such as Christensen and Larsen Co., and Johannes Hansen Co.

While not directly related to this book, the staff of the Danish Embassy, especially Ambassador Fleming Hedego and his wife and Mr. Bents Lindblad, were always helpful and sponsored exhibitions on Danish chairs.

I found that some people only wanted to know how many chairs were in the research collection. While some people only think of these chairs as assets, I feel that the real value of the chairs is in the friends they have brought me. Without my research, I would never have met these people and would have had an unexceptional life. Though I have sacrificed much on account of these chairs, my sacrifices have been returned tenfold. I have really been researching people's residences as well as chairs, and I was lucky in having two such subjects for my life's work.

My work could never have continued without all the assistance provided by these people. I can never fully express my appreciation—and apology—to the staff of my illustration office in particular, for whom I caused immeasurable trouble and burdens. I hope they will forgive me for my selfishness.

When we were designing this publication, we wanted to show the chairs from four directions, as in the records of the Finn Juhl Yuuru Memorial in 1990. We wished to make this book valuable as an information source. Unfortunately, this would have been an expensive and enormous work to produce and we were forced to condense that information into the current volume when our prepared draft was too big.

Finally, this small space is hardly sufficient to thank the people who have assisted us with photography and in transporting and storing the furniture.

My sincere thanks to two Sensei's: Architect Dan Miyawaki and Professor Shin Shimazaki of Musashino Art College, who led me into this wonderful world of chairs.

And we thank Mr. Tsutom Nishioka for his work in the design and layout of the book and Inoue and Ms. Masuko Okubo from Korinsha Publishing for the editing. Thank you very much.

ACKNOWLEDGMENTS

A/S FREDERICIA STOLEFABRIK
CARL HANSEN & SØN
DANISH DESIGN COUNCIL
DANISH TRADE OFFICE
DEN PARMANENTE A/S
FRITZ HANSENS EFTF. A/S
GETAMA A/S
JOHANNES HANSEN A/S
MAGNUS OLESEN A/S
PP MØBLER
ROYAL DANISH EMBASSY
ROYAL FURNITURE COLLECTION
RUD. RASMUSSENS SNEDKERIER
THE ROYAL ACADEMY OF FINE ARTS

Andersen, Kazue Holst
Andersen, Yuki Holst
Andersen, Niels Roth
Asmussen, A. P.
Bernsen, Jens
Bjerregaard, Birgitte
Bjerregaard, Kirsten
Buhl, Charlotte
Ditzel, Nanna
Gjaerlov-Knudsen, Ole
Gudiksen, Marno
Hansen, Poul
Hansen, Roald Steen
Hedegaard, Flemming
Jalk, Grete
Jensen, Sumiko
Jeppesen, Peter
Juhl, Finn
Khaerholm, Hanne
Krogh, Erik
Lindgrad, Bent
Matz, Søren
Matz, Tom
Møller, Henrik Stern
Neupert, Jacqes
Nygaard, Jul
Oertoft, Niels
Olesen, Kjeld
Pedersen, Ejner
Risvang, Søren
Rud. Rasmussen, Jørgen
Romer, Mike
Sieck, Frederik
Skov, Torben
Stokholm, Taeko
Staerk, Peter
Sørensen, Johnny
Thanild, Benni
Thygesen, Rud
Wegner, Hans J.
Wegner, Marianne
Wilhelm Hansen, Hanne

INDEX